10 X CULTURE

THE 4-HOUR MEETING WEEK AND 25 OTHER
SECRETS FROM INNOVATIVE, FAST-MOVING
TEAMS

ROB LENNON   JOSH LOWY   DARREN CHAIT

HUGO PRESS

This book is given to_____ because I want you
and your team to thrive.

Read on your favorite device or share with a friend at **www.hugo.team/10x**.

PRINTED IN THE UNITED STATES OF AMERICA
FIRST PRINTING, 2019 BY HUGO PRESS
COVER ILLUSTRATION BY ZOË VAN DIJK
EDITED BY JOSIAH WARTAK

ISBN 978-0-578-58494-2

For printing and publishing inquiries, contact us at **hello@hugo.team**.

Visit us online at **www.hugo.team**

CONTENTS

FOREWORD BY ERIC S. YUAN, CEO AT ZOOM

When I was a freshman in college, my girlfriend lived a ten-hour train ride away. I could only visit her twice a year, which was really hard on both of us. On one of those long rides, I started imagining a device that I could use to see her — to talk to her — like we were both in the same room.

I thought the hard part of my idea would be the technology, the team, the business model, or the investors. But later, as vice president of engineering at a massive technology company, I found that assumption to be wrong. Even with all of those things in place, the customers I talked to were still unhappy and frustrated with the collaboration software they were using.

So when I started Zoom, I sat in my tiny shared office and thought about the culture I wanted this new company to have. I decided that our company culture should be based around one thing: happiness. My dream I wanted to build — a place for people to come together on video, and speak, face-to-face — would be a failure if it didn't deliver happiness.

From that day, the foundation for our culture became delivering happiness to each other and to our customers. Customer happiness starts with employee happiness. I needed to make sure that I was happy, and that my employees were happy, or we would fail at our mission.

That's how I discovered the hardest part of building my idea: It was creating the right culture in every part of the company. It's just not something we could figure out on our own. You can't just tell people to care about each other. And you cannot force people to be happy.

There was no happiness manual we could read. There was no roadmap to building a happiness culture. Creating the company culture we wanted took careful thought, reading, and experimentation. We made it our priority.

The book you hold in your hands is the manual I wish I had a decade ago. It is packed with engaging narrative, compelling research, and rare psychological insight into the culture-building process. On these pages, you will find many of the lessons I learned the hard way building Zoom over the last eight years.

Culture is the most important — and hardest — element of building a company. If your culture is off, even if you make good progress, it will not be sustainable. And once you have a culture problem, it's very hard to fix. It has to be a Day 1 priority.

With this book, you have a guide to the entire process of building a culture. At Zoom, we have used these principles to successfully establish a culture of happiness and caring — and to build a successful company with happy customers.

For the sake of your coworkers, your customers, your community, your company, and yourself, read this book — because I know that having a strong culture on your team will bring you happiness, as it has for me, and everyone who has helped build Zoom into what it is today.

Eric S. Yuan
Founder & CEO, Zoom

I

PILLARS OF A 10X
CULTURE

In writing this book, we wanted to share our most profound insights into what we've learned and what our customers have taught us while building a successful business. So why did we choose to focus on culture — not strategy, or management, or marketing?

When we looked at every technique, tactic, and factor that has influenced our success, nothing has had more impact than teamwork and team culture. As management guru Peter Drucker said, "Culture eats strategy for breakfast."

Getting culture wrong is more detrimental than missing the mark on any one strategy. No matter how clever your product is or how high-growth your industry, you will not get ahead if your team is dysfunctional.

And the opposite is also true: A strong team culture can withstand missteps on the path to success.

In our journey at Hugo to build a 10X Culture — a culture that enabled us to 10X our company in record time — we've studied a range of industries. We have learned lessons from the stories of groundbreaking companies such as Zoom, Atlassian, and Slack.

We studied the workings of secret (and not-so-secret) labs attacking problems the world has never before tried to solve. We closely observed the world's best global enterprises. Again and again, we were confronted by a commonality that stood out among all winners and losers.

Yes, you may have a better product. Maybe you're better positioned to win in your market. But all of the great endeavors of the last two centuries have not been accomplished solely because of an excellent strategy in winning market conditions. They have been **team-driven**.

It doesn't matter if you're just starting out, in a next-level growth cycle for your business, or are a market leader responding to new conditions. You cannot effectively solve higher-order problems unless teamwork is thriving.

Companies that add drag to collaboration, empowerment, and autonomy find it a slog to generate results. If you fail to connect the way you operate to the factors that make humans thrive — call it *team-culture fit* — you'll cap your team's potential instead of unleashing it.

In our fast-moving, tech-enabled world, successful teams win because they are able to harness their full potential — not only the potential of each member, but the synergistic power of them all. When we talk about 10X Culture in this book, that is the kind of culture we're talking about: a culture that empowers teams and drives business outcomes.

From feats like rebuilding our entire website in forty-five days to doubling daily active users month over month, we've repeatedly proven that *the way you work* can be an incredible competitive advantage.

A 10X Culture results in teamwork that pushes the business to outperform all others in a way that, when viewed from within the confines of a traditional team, seems *impossible*.

We'll show you through examples of the greatest teams of our era — and some of our own experiences with our 10X team — how to cultivate and reinforce this kind of working environment in your company to achieve similar results.

10X Culture is also about building a culture where humans thrive. When you unleash human potential, both individually and collaboratively, outcomes from those same people, with the same amount of time, resources, and skills, dramatically increase.

When your entire team is informed, motivated, and enthusiastic, you're unstoppable. You're 10X.

This is not another management book rehashing age-old strategies and approaches. We *will* look to the past to rediscover some of the most successful lessons that were somehow forgotten. But many traditional strategies — aspects of work that you may have considered immutable laws of nature — simply won't work the way they used to. They actually hold you back. Why?

The modern workforce is diverse, distributed, and flexible. The very nature of work has changed, and we must change with it. This book explores the factors that drive autonomy, empowerment, agility, and urgency in modern workplaces. It will teach you practical strategies to ingrain these qualities in your team culture.

And because of the synergistic nature of empowerment, when you build a business with amazing teamwork and empowering culture, your company is capable of results that are an order of magnitude greater than you would otherwise see.

Welcome to the future of teamwork: 10X Culture.

1

"DON'T F*#K UP THE CULTURE"

IT IS late 2012 in San Francisco. Fall in the Bay Area is hot — somehow warmer than the summer. The executive team at Airbnb is hunkered down in the "Berlin" room at their headquarters. They have just closed $150 million in a Series C funding round with Peter Thiel, the founder of PayPal and Palantir.

With the AC humming, they are reviewing Airbnb's metrics. The conversation is casual — sometimes comical — with that character-istic informality that had turned the notion of an air mattress in some-one's living room into a global phenomenon.

Midway through the conversation, Brian Chesky, co-founder and CEO of Airbnb, stops. He probably turns away from the projector, his face softening as he asks Thiel a simple question:

"What is the single most important piece of advice you have for us?"

Peter Thiel replies sharply, in his signature outspoken manner, without taking even a second to consider possible responses.

"Don't f#k up the culture."*

Airbnb was already hauling in hundreds of millions of dollars in revenue a year. Despite this initial success, they were dwarfed by incumbent companies in a colossal hotel market. $450 million was only 0.1% market share.

Reflecting on the moment a year later, Brian wrote:

> *When the culture is strong, you can trust everyone to do the right thing. People can be independent and autonomous. They can be entrepreneurial. And if we have a company that is entrepreneurial in spirit, we will be able to take our next '(wo)man on the moon' leap.*

Current projections indicate that Airbnb's revenue in 2020 will be $8.5 billion — 18X what it was when Peter gave his advice.

The "(wo)man on the moon"[1] leap that Brian refers to epitomizes 10X Culture. Whether or not he knew it at the time, getting there would require many of the same aspects of team culture that made the original Apollo mission a success.

—

IN THE EXTENSIVE training and planning before the 1969 Apollo 11 launch, the three astronauts who would participate in the original moon landing couldn't have been more different.

Neil Armstrong was known for his brooding, emotionally remote personality. Buzz Aldrin was sarcastic, often abrasive — able to defeat you instantly with a biting remark. Michael Collins, by contrast, was described as "happy-go-lucky" by his peers.

Yet these three, who were not close friends, backed by a team of more than 300,000 people across the private and public sectors, executed one of the most extreme, complex missions ever undertaken by humankind.

After the mission, Armstrong attributed its success to being "a project in which everybody was . . . interested . . . involved . . . and fascinated by the job they were doing." The Apollo team was motivated "to [do] their job a little better than they have to."

Landing on the moon wasn't simply a victory of intellect and ability by talented people; it was the outcome of a motivated workforce with a culture of success.

You don't need to be best friends with your colleagues in order to be an effective leader. You do need to accept who your colleagues are and foster an environment in which everyone's contributions are able to be unleashed.

—

WITH APOLLO 11, the real, hidden story was the way that they innovated on teamwork and collaboration in order to pull off such a complex endeavor. How could so many people work so well together — especially on a government-led project in an era not known for its cultivation of teamwork?

That question led us to other stories of similar feats. The Manhattan Project's attempts to produce the world's first atomic bomb necessitated substantial bets (just like today's startups) and innovations in teamwork.

In this century, coalition forces in Iraq initially found themselves losing bitterly, despite having advantages in manpower and technology. Traditional processes, teamwork, and even military culture turned out to be woefully underpowered versus agile, adaptable terrorist cells. One of the most rigid organizations in the modern world had to find a way to transform their culture into one that could win despite constantly changing circumstances.

You might be skeptical about how applicable these scenarios are to your own challenges. You're not trying to invent the atomic bomb or land on the moon. You're just trying to build a business or manage your team in the midst of the digital age.

But since these expansive endeavors, a *to-the-moon* level of complexity has become the status quo for every organization. The rise of the Internet, big data, hardware improvements, and everything else that followed, has ingrained a level of complexity into businesses and teams that, frankly, wasn't as big of an issue before the computer age.

Today's smartphones are millions of times faster than the Apollo Guidance Computer of the 1960s. While this means your phone can be a tool to solve problems infinitely faster than Apollo's computers, others on their phones are out there adding complexity to your world at the same pace.

The success of all of these projects of the past — as well as many more from our current age — is often mistakenly attributed wholly to the brilliant minds of those who are a part of them. It's as if being clever and smart is all that is required.

Yes, exceptional people certainly often accomplish exceptional feats. But there are far more talented individuals who do not have the support of a team that allows their work to thrive and flourish. Simply put, these teams were able to accomplish world firsts because of their values and cultures.

When we closely examine the successful teams of the past and present, we can identify the distinct ways in which these people operate — ways that differ from and sometimes directly conflict with the status quo of teamwork. Teams that successfully take (wo)man on the moon leaps share three traits. They are *adaptable, networked,* and *tempo-oriented.*

---

1. NASA plans to land the first woman on the moon in 2024. Perhaps Brian was so tapped into our country's astronomical endeavors that he chose a metaphor that would become a reality during his company's meteoric rise.

2

HEART OF A 10X TEAM

BEFORE WE GET into the nuts and bolts of how to produce a 10X Culture in your team, we'll examine the key traits of a 10X team and why they're so important.

The journey to a 10X Culture begins with change. The path any organization will need to take is uncertain. So to get there in one piece, you're going to need to be adaptable.

Adaptable

It became the most famous monologue in action movie history. In the blockbuster *Taken*, Liam Neeson played ex–special forces operative Brian Mills. It's hard not to hear his voice in your head as you relive the scene where he gets on the phone with the guys who kidnapped his daughter:

> *What I do have are a very particular set of skills, skills I have acquired over a very long career, skills that make me a nightmare for people like you. If you let my daughter go now, that'll be the end of it. I will not look for*

you. I will not pursue you. But if you don't, I will look for
you. I will find you. And I will kill you.

What are these skills he's talking about? Hand-to-hand combat. Expert marksmanship. Explosives. Stealthy movement. Liam Neeson can do it all.

But more than anything else, what makes his character so dangerous in these movies is Neeson's relentless adaptability. He doesn't know who has taken his daughter, where they are, or what they want. He's going to have to figure that out. His predicament is incredibly uncertain. But he is prepared for uncertainty.

The secret to success in our uncertain, modern world is not a specific belief or skill. It's the ability to rapidly change beliefs and develop skills based on an evolving, uncertain environment. As Lt. Colonel John Boyd said, "He who can handle the quickest rate of change survives."

The rate of change is only getting faster, which has spawned clichés like *every company is a technology company*, later adapted to *every company is a software company*.

Companies like Ford are tackling this problem head on. "Bill Ford said recently that when he was growing up he used to worry about making more cars," said Venkatesh Prasad, a senior technical leader at Ford. "Now he worries — what if we only made more cars? Just making more cars is not our future." Instead, Ford is reinventing itself as a maker of "sophisticated computers-on-wheels."

But what if, unlike Ford, you're already a technology or software company? Competition is still rising all around you. Threats to your business aren't a matter of strategy or luck — they're just a matter of time. And when market conditions change, if you don't adapt fast enough, you might never recover.

How do you make your organization more *adaptable*? A common feature of adaptable teams is how they plan. To be adaptable, you must be willing to change plans. To do it successfully, you must be able to change plans without sacrificing alignment.

Put simply, this is the approach we learned from other high-growth companies that has served us well: Plan for *alignment*, not commitment.

Begin by setting up a forum for re-evaluation. At Hugo, we subscribe to a four-hour meeting limit per week for internal meetings (for more on how we do that, see Chapter 19). We cap the amount of time that team members should spend in scheduled internal meetings. This maximizes productivity and gives the team a lot of control over their own time.

To balance all this time that we invest in execution, we schedule a regular forum for revisiting our plans. We call it a HiLo[1]. We look to see how the market and environment has changed, and discuss whether we should stay the course or depart from the plan based on new information. We remain adaptable, but are less tempted to rethink strategy and decisions on a whim.

We agree on the criteria, as a team, for when we should change our plans. We do this using these three questions:

1. Do we have new information that we didn't have when we made the decision?
2. Would changing course likely have an impact on our desired outcomes?
3. How does the original rationale we used hold up against today's information?

How often does your team have the opportunity to look out, re-evaluate, and consider adapting? Doing so too often leads to a lack of focus that undermines your ability to execute. But doing so too rarely prevents you from being flexible as an organization.

The need for adaptability in the workplace isn't exactly a secret. In 2018, more than 90 percent of HR experts said that their major criteria for recruitment was the ability of a candidate to adapt[2].

If you want to adapt, you must know what to adapt to and why it's important. To do that, you must first open your mind.

Networked

Individuals, teams, cities, and even nations thrive when they are parts of open systems. If they close themselves off, they suffocate, condemning themselves to obsolescence or irrelevance.

It's not good enough just to be an open workplace. You must be networked — both open *and* connected.

This may seem counterintuitive, because connection seems as though it is inevitable. Technology has enabled people to be in constant contact. It practically mandates it. Whereas other teams may find connectedness a burden, what sets 10X teams apart is their ability to use their interconnectedness to amplify their capabilities.

There's an interesting paradox at play here. Becoming more open and connected is actually becoming *more* difficult as we adopt technology.

The average organization uses 123 different SaaS tools[3] across all of its departments. This leads to massive data fragmentation as each team uses products dedicated specifically to their needs.

In addition, the remote and distributed nature of organizations today causes a second type of fragmentation: people fragmentation. More than 70 percent of modern teams are remote, at least in part. As I write this, I'm sitting in my home office more than one thousand miles away from my nearest coworker.

Being a networked organization allows you to reap the gains of having disparate tools and workers without suffering all the downside of fragmentation. Here are a few concepts to offset this fragmentation, and in turn maximize openness and connectedness, that have been very effective for our customers and the companies we work with every day.

Adopt tools that talk. When selecting tools, assign a greater weight to integration and sync potential between systems — especially those that involve workflow and process. In our company, we don't use tools that can't communicate as a single stack. Not every tool integrates with every other tool, but every element in our foundational stack touches just about everything else.

That means communication and project management tools sync with Slack. Any development tools connect to Github. We're stitch systems together with Zapier if they don't talk to each other. And our own product, Hugo, allows meeting insights and action items to be transferred to any system in which we do planning or task management, be it Salesforce, Jira, Asana, or any one of twenty other tools.

Optimize for high-bandwidth communication. Bandwidth isn't just a term used to describe your internet connection. Bandwidth is simply a broad measure of how much information you can transmit or receive in a given time period.

Think about how much easier it is to convey a message in person versus in writing. Verbal communication is high-bandwidth. Written communication is low-bandwidth. The order of bandwidth by communication channel is as follows:

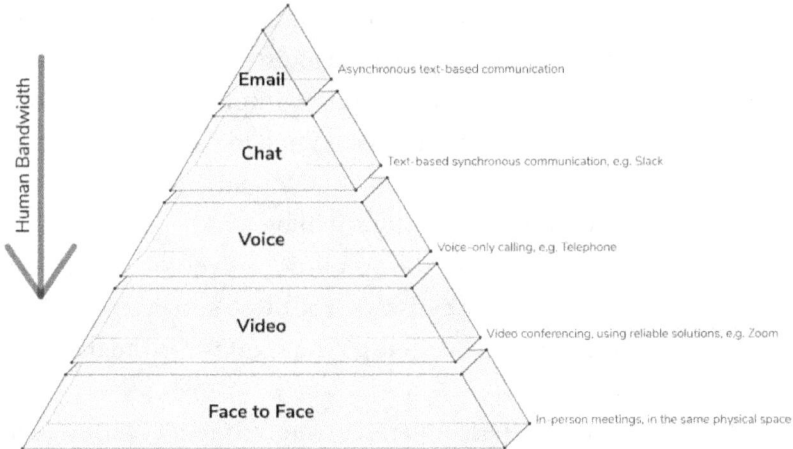

One of Zoom's values that we identify with is to use video as often as possible, because it enables the most genuine human interactions. But the value of seeing someone's face goes far beyond relationship-building. So much of communication is nonverbal; seeing someone's facial expressions and movements reveals much more information than simply hearing or seeing their words.

Recorded video is also powerful because it is asynchronous — it can be watched on demand and doesn't require two people to be free at the same time — which has been incredibly powerful for our distributed team where distance and time zones present communication challenges. It's also far faster to record a quick three-minute video rather than stress over writing a detailed email for fifteen minutes.

At Hugo, we have found video to be so efficient and impactful that we hacked together an internal product for recording videos that self-destruct after seven days. We call it Fade[4], and it allows anyone to record a video for any reason, without having to worry about whether the video is *good*.

From adopting software systems that talk to each other to having real-time, asynchronous communication, the workplace is flush with opportunities to be more connected.

Like lighter fluid on a fire, connectedness ignites what is already present. If your workplace is toxic, the tools you use to stay connected will make it more toxic. But when your workplace is full of teams that are motivated, informed, and interested in a higher purpose, the more connected and open you are with your team and tools, the greater the impact of your decisions and actions will be.

Connectedness increases the amplitude of your actions, for better or worse. To improve the effectiveness of those activities over the long term, you must increase your tempo: how often you make decisions and act on them.

As your connectedness increases, the frequency with which you take actions becomes more important. If you don't increase your tempo to match the volume of information you are being presented with, you will fall more behind.

Tempo-Oriented

A lot of ink has been spilled on why startups and younger businesses are able to outcompete incumbents. The number one reason given is almost always *speed*, but that's a misnomer.

The real answer is *tempo*.

Tempo is the rate at which you perform a movement or series of actions. Speed is the net time that elapses. So tempo a way to increase your rate of motion without rushing your work. Here's an example.

Want to shoot faster? Increase the tempo with which you shoot, not your speed.

The difference is simple: When shooting, the fastest, most accurate shooters pull the trigger slowly and consistently. Then they release the trigger as quickly as possible. They only take their time with the part of the movement that needs to be performed carefully, without wasting a second on the time between shots.

The equivalent principle for businesses like ours is to maximize the frequency with which you perform core activities.

It's not as important to focus on all of the activities you perform generally. Improve your team's performance by optimizing for tempo in the areas that matter most.

Working faster, smarter, better — in just a few aspects of your work — can pay off big. The compounding effect of this is absolutely tremendous.

As a thought experiment, let's assume that every time your team culture makes something better at work, it's a 1 percent improvement. Doing things 1 percent better is achievable, right? *Right*.

Now, let's bring in the tempo factor. Achieving a 1 percent better result every day doesn't sound like much. But after one year of daily improvements, you end up with a 3,778 percent gain.

When you orient around increasing your tempo, you improve by 1 percent more often. The faster the tempo gets, the greater the compounding improvements.

Many teams don't think about tempo as a way to unlock effectiveness in their organizations. But what you will find is that having an incredible team culture encourages a higher frequency of action, and is actually the secret to fully unleashing your potential.

Here's one way to optimize tempo: Begin by identifying a project, process, or experiment that is being carried out by your team. Draw a quick timeline, estimating the time requirement of each step.

Now categorize each step:

1. Is the time frame under your control?
2. Is the time frame impacted by external factors?
3. Is there a cost associated with reducing the time allocated?

If you answered yes, no, and no, that indicates you have an opportunity to release the trigger faster between shots and increase your tempo.

Here's an example. This year, the Hugo team agreed that updating our website was a high priority. In my experience, that's usually a three-to-six-month project at best. It includes user research, copywriting, product positioning, wireframing and design, development, QA, SEO . . . the list goes on.

So how were we able to create and launch a new website in forty-five days? We focused on tempo.

- We booked ten user research sessions over two days to identify the trends and insights as quickly as we could.
- We made sure our team had everything needed to develop the site in a short sprint.
- All of our QA test cases were defined so that two people could rapidly test the entire site in just a few hours.
- We let messaging, design, and SEO take the other forty-one days. We didn't worry about timing for these critical steps, as they were either out of our control or required that much time to be executed successfully.

You can see how we applied the heuristic outlined above in the following chart:

Step	In our control?	Impacted by external factors?	Cost to reduce time?
User research	Yes (assuming we have enough users to reach out to who are available quickly)	No	No
Messaging experimentation	Yes	Yes (We need enough new visitors to come to the website)	N/A
Wireframing / UX design	Yes	No	Yes (If we accept that less time to iterate and explore design = suboptimal design outcomes.)
Illustration / visual design	Yes	No	Yes
Development	Yes	No	No (Our dev team is adaptable. Quality doesn't suffer under pressure.)
QA / Testing	Yes	No	No (We have test cases defined, so we can just run through them faster.)
SEO	No	Yes (we can't tell Google to increase our rankings on our schedule)	N/A

This framework is just one example of how we operate at an incredibly high tempo, but not necessarily speed — depending on the project.

These team attributes — being adaptable, networked, and tempo-oriented — provide a clear picture of the end result we're aiming for. The remainder of this book covers practical strategies and solutions for creating this kind of culture on your team.

We're going to explore topics such as leadership, hiring, customer interactions, and meetings. All of these involve one activity — something that is central to running a business. It's something that you do every day: decision-making.

1. HiLo refers to zooming out and zooming in together. We look at strategy, progress, and discuss existential topics, while also zooming into specific tactics and small wins.
2. Deloitte (2019). 2019 Global Human Capital Trends. Retrieved from https://www2.deloitte.com/insights/us/en/focus/human-capital-trends.html
3. Blissfully (2019). 2019 SaaS Trends. Retrieved from https://martechtoday.com/new-blissfully-report-most-companies-have-orphaned-saas-apps-in-their-stacks-231064
4. Sign up to use Fade for yourself at www.hugo.team/fade

SUMMARY: PILLARS OF A 10X CULTURE

- Today's companies face a (*wo*)*man-on-the-moon* level of complexity and uncertainty. This necessitates approaches to teamwork that previously were only required by the world's greatest endeavors.
- When your team culture is **adaptable**, you are able to process new information and change course without losing focus.
- You must be **networked** because technology has created a crisis of data fragmentation and people fragmentation — a situation you can turn to your advantage by choosing tools that talk to each other and by optimizing for high-bandwidth communication.
- Increase your team's rate of progress without rushing your work by increasing the **tempo** with which you perform actions that are within your control and that have little-to-no cost for reducing time.

II

10X DECISION-MAKING

When Mike Cannon-Brookes and Scott Farquhar founded Atlassian, all they had was a pile of good ideas and a credit card with a $10,000 limit. Farquhar said his initial management philosophy was based on his co-op internship experiences and those of his former classmates. For him, managing was more about what *not* to do than what *to* do.

"When we would go to lunch with friends who had joined other companies, the biggest problem we found was that they thought their managers were idiots in some ways," Farquhar said. "More than that, our friends had no mechanism to make a change. They always felt that they weren't empowered. I told Mike, 'Shit, I hope no one ever leaves Atlassian and goes to their lunchtimes and bitches about how they can't get stuff done.'"

Not being able to get stuff done is a symptom. At its root lies the larger problem of not being able to make decisions. Any competent person is able to do their job — provided they are empowered to do so. So it makes sense that we continue our journey into 10X Culture by looking at how decisions are made, both within and across teams.

Decision-making is impacted by almost every aspect of how you work. Decisions can either be constrained or unleashed by your internal processes. Because of this, you can train yourself and your team to make better decisions, faster. Above all, decision-making relies heavily on relationships and cultural norms on your team, and whether you're emotionally and intellectually connected.

3

CULTIVATE A SHARED
CONSCIOUSNESS

RETIRED U.S. ARMY GENERAL STANLEY MCCHRYSTAL knows a little about building teams. During his command of Joint Special Operations Command (JSOC) in the mid-2000s, he created alignment and comradery between disparate — and often antagonistic — branches of the military and transformed them into a cohesive fighting force capable of moving with the same speed and flexibility of Al Qaeda forces in the Middle East.

In a talk on teamwork to Stanford GSB students in 2014, McChrystal sited the failure of the 2004 U.S. "dream team" — a group of world-class basketball players that paired young stars such as LeBron James, Dwayne Wade, and Anthony Carmelo with veteran MVPs such as Tim Duncan and Allen Iverson. Believed to be unbeatable in the Olympics because of their overwhelming talent and skill, the team was ultimately knocked out by Argentina in a huge upset. They finished with a disappointing bronze medal.

The "lesser" teams that beat them played "more like teams," McChrystal said. "Talent alone doesn't make a great team. You need faith in your colleagues and alignment behind a common goal." Faith, trust, and alignment boils down to what McChrystal calls a *shared consciousness*, which was a critical component in how he turned the tide against Al Qaeda.

You might envision this idea similar to a state of "flow," where you become immersed in a task or project. Now imagine that same flow state applying to your team dynamic.

Shared consciousness enables you to read, anticipate, and even nonverbally communicate with your team members. It results in "emergent intelligence and awareness" that optimizes the adaptable, networked, tempo-oriented nature of effective teams. Even when your team isn't immediately around you, shared consciousness enables you to act as if they are — anticipating how they will think, approach, and react to various challenges.

A major component of shared consciousness is *having mutual trust*. When you are working with people you trust, you all move more quickly because you have confidence in each other. It's a relationship of ease and freedom. Instead of burning calories looking over your shoulder, you can focus on what's in front of you. Think of a time when the opposite was true and you worked with people you didn't trust. How much time and effort did you waste just trying to prevent them from messing something up?

Trust can be cultivated. In work, there are two major factors to earning and creating mutual trust:

1. **Core values** – Having a common purpose that includes a shared perspective and worldview.
2. **Experience** – Overcoming difficult, complex situations together.

Trust within a team means you don't have to micromanage each other. You know your teammates will either achieve success on their own or come to you if they need something. You can focus on your own objectives, and they will trust you in kind.

Mutual trust is earned and amplified with actions you take from the beginning of the hiring process to your last day at work. The important idea to understand now is that trust-building is a component of every activity and action. It's not something you decide; it's something you *do*.

Here are four actionable ideas for increasing mutual trust, the basis for shared consciousness on your team.

Experience other roles

The global food chain McDonald's requires new corporate hires to flip burgers at a restaurant for their first few weeks on the job. Here's the thinking behind that decision: How can the new hires drive corporate strategy, manage legal compliance, or market the brand if they've never experienced what work in their restaurants is like? Slipping into other roles than the ones they normally work in will help them understand their coworkers' and customers' challenges.

Why shouldn't your marketing team take the occasional support ticket to know what customers have trouble doing? Engineering can do the same, to get a sense of the bugs being reported. There are many ways to orchestrate this, and all of them help build trust. As issues arise, team members who have experienced other jobs firsthand will better understand the tradeoffs and challenges their co-workers are facing.

Build cross-functional teams

Teams that consistently work together, with similar skills and overlapping tasks, are much more likely to be well coordinated. What about teams that aren't so close? Your goal is to create shared consciousness across your organization — even among teammates who don't operate in this way.

Eradicate internal silos by building teams made up of people from different functions wherever possible. We've seen great marketing ideas come from engineers, and technical solutions come from marketers, too. Collaborate across roles often enough, and you might be surprised at the result. By working in tandem to reach common goals, teams will develop heightened emotional and intellectual connections, which in turn lead to the bonds that enable shared consciousness.

Develop "battle rhythms"

Creating predictable, frequent rhythms allows groups to better synchronize their activities, and in turn develop a common way of thinking. McChrystal calls these *battle rhythms*. They include four processes which are often done ad hoc but deserve to have their own rhythms:

1. Planning for the future
2. Deciding what to do
3. Monitoring projects and processes
4. Assessing what worked and what didn't

To implement battle rhythms of your own, think about your business routines. Do you make consistent time for each activity? Many companies plan on a quarterly basis, make decisions when necessary, look at a process only when it is broken, and never have retrospectives.

At Hugo, we've been guilty of the same sins. That's why we use battle rhythms so that we don't fall into bad habits again by accident — which is always a possibility when you're moving fast and work gets busy — so we re-sync on a weekly basis. This isn't just for information transparency; it's a predictable rhythm.

Maximize sharing

To create an environment in which your peers can think like you, they need to know everything relevant that you know. There are many ways to do this, and almost all of them boil down to the idea of *sharing.* As you seek to share consciousness, you'll first need to share *information.*

Sounds simple, right? But one of the types of information that often doesn't get shared is how you approach problems and make decisions. Problem-solving involves a fantastic amount of knowledge, including:

- What you know about a topic
- What external resources or data you rely on
- What your assumptions are
- How you interpret information
- What mental models you apply to certain problems
- What you expect to happen

As you can see, this is a veritable case study on your brain. So to start, one of the best ways to make *how you think* more transparent, and give coworkers access to experiences they weren't involved in, is with a shared decision log.

4

KEEP A SHARED DECISION LOG

A NUMBER of challenges we've covered so far relate to the complexity that comes from overwhelming amounts of information. A constant torrent of new data and trends, dispersed across people and tools, makes it seem impossible to achieve these traits that 10X teams have — being adaptable, networked, and operating at optimal tempo.

A shift in the way that you and your team approaches decision-making, however, will make this impossible goal suddenly appear within reach. You'll be surprised at how huge the improvement in outcomes can be.

The foundations of a shared decision log

At Hugo, we sat down to figure out an approach to decision-making that optimizes for speed and decentralization. To do so, we asked ourselves these questions:

- How can we empower more people to make their own decisions without having to seek permission first?

- How can we reduce the number of people involved in each decision?
- When new information is generated, how do we encourage past decisions to be reassessed and adjusted?

It seemed that the real reason we were ensuring decision oversight at every step was to prevent people from moving away from core goals and values. If decisions aren't aligned with business goals, customer goals, and each other's goals, then allowing more people to make decisions more often only creates problems. We wanted an open team process that would be an effective antidote to misalignment, but without requiring oversight.

If you're familiar with product design, you may be familiar with the idea of the "spec." It's basically a document that outlines what an engineer is going to build. Often, there are edge cases that get left off the spec because they aren't immediately noticed. A good engineer, and one who is operating with shared consciousness, knows that the edge cases are important — and they fill in those gaps on their own.

What if we took that idea — that people should be empowered to make decisions that relate to their work — and expanded on it?

Based on that question, we made a rule: If you think it's necessary to make a decision, you can make it. You don't even need to talk to anyone else about it if you don't think you need to. But if it's an important decision, you've got to write it down, along with a future review date to compare what you expected to happen with the actual outcome.

The resulting decision log is designed to help everyone achieve shared consciousness. Think of it as a tool to help finish each other's sentences. When everyone on the team has the right balance of awareness for what others are working on and what they care about day-to-day, then they can start to act on behalf of one another automatically.

We didn't pioneer the idea of a decision log, but we did build on it. We've made it a habit for everyone, so that anyone in the team can log decisions whenever it makes sense to do so.

Reviewing the decision log is also a shared activity. We share our logs in team meetings so that over time we can build horizontal awareness. Marketing starts to appreciate the challenges and focus of our engineering team, and vice versa. Because of this, we can all run much more accurate simulations in our heads of how other team-mates think and what they care about. We can evaluate how past actions have improved or worsened business outcomes. And we can support each other automatically by understanding each other's points of view.

Combining decentralized decision-making with the decision log enables your team to dramatically increase both tempo and output without impairing overall alignment. It also bolsters another trait of 10X work: *autonomy*.

Most companies — intentionally or not — have a culture that discourages autonomy. This bad practice comes from management philosophies that date back to industrialization. A manager's role was historically to make all of the important decisions and hold the knowledge. Workers were just to do their jobs. But over the last hundred years, technology has ushered in a change to the nature of most work which has evolved to ask much more from those performing it. In most professions, you are, to some degree or another, both the manager *and* the worker. Rather than simply assembling cogs and widgets in a predefined way, each of us is building our own tiny new machines every day.

You might not specifically ascribe to that old-fashioned way of working. But you probably still believe that decisions, especially if they're important, need to be run by the higher-ups — even if those same higher-ups are not the best informed to be making those decisions.

Let's return to our example engineer. She spends hours pondering how to code a feature, and comes up with an idea to solve the problem in the most effective way. She brings her solution to her manager, who used to code every day but now mostly works with people. What are the chances that the manager is going to say no? Zero. Our coder is the subject matter expert. With or without a decision log, she was always going to make the decision.

In addition to removing multiple hoops that need to be jumped through for obvious decisions, having a decision log allows team members to see how each other thinks. By having to write out the rationale behind your decision, you expose each other to not just the decision, but also the thought process behind it.

This is often an even greater asset to the company than the autonomy that such a decision log grants. Over time, team members will develop new ways of thinking based on what they have seen from the decisions of others. In fact, subordinates will get much better at making decisions using the same thought processes and criteria that their managers might have used, having seen time after time how these kinds of decisions are made.

Daniel Kahneman, who won the Nobel Prize for his work on the psychology of judgement and decision-making, promotes a decision log as a way to eliminate hindsight bias:

> *Whenever you're making a consequential decision . . . just take a moment to think, write down what you expect to happen, why you expect it to happen and . . . write down how you feel about the situation, both physically and even emotionally. Just, how do you feel?*

Every day, in every company, people make decisions that relate to their work. In order to begin developing your 10X Culture, we propose that you empower every person to be able to make any decision they feel they should be able to make on their own — without approval.

However, all decisions made in this way — in a vacuum, if you will — must be logged publicly, along with the following information:

1. The rationale behind the decision
2. The expected outcome
3. How the employee feels about the situation
4. A date to revisit the decision and see what happened

When you do this, you begin to identify biases in your thought process, and become more effective in decision-making. You'll also benefit from the decisions of others by being exposed to new mental models which you can then apply to your own challenges.

A decision log is an example of *proactive sharing*, a communication strategy that enables everyone in your organization to be in the know. Instead of waiting for information to come to you, you can empower everyone with information they didn't even know they needed to learn.

This decision opens up a whole new slew of questions: How much information is the right amount? What should you share? What shouldn't you?

5

ACCELERATE KNOWLEDGE TRANSFER

WHAT's the best way to grow mushrooms? *Keep them in the dark and feed them bullshit.*

The same phrase could summarize the knowledge-sharing strategy of some managers who insist on keeping workers under-informed with incomplete or inaccurate information. Except people — unlike our delicious fungi friends — don't respond so well to being kept in the dark.

The metaphor works on multiple levels. Mushrooms are top-heavy and only thrive in specific conditions — damp, dark ones. Innovative teams, by contrast, are evenly distributed and widely adaptable. So check yourself if you're treating the people around you like mushrooms — especially when it comes to what and how you share.

In 2015, Geckoboard and Censuswide surveyed 2000 employees of UK and U.S. businesses to learn about the "mushroom management" phenomenon[1]. Their research uncovered a striking relationship between information sharing and employee engagement.

- Over 80 percent of employees want leadership to share more information about the business

- One in four employees know someone who has left a business — or have left themselves — due to a lack of transparency in business direction and performance
- Over 50 percent of employees say that more company information and data being shared had a large, positive impact on both their productivity and performance

There are many understandable reasons for leaders withholding information. They may be concerned that it will weaken their position in the company. They may feel too busy to share it. They may not even be aware that something could be shared, or should be. But all of these excuses are symptoms of not being adaptable, networked, and tempo-oriented. All can be overcome.

While a lack of information sharing can be a major detractor to the workplace environment, the opposite also holds true. Proactively sharing information is one of the easiest steps toward creating a trusting and motivated workforce. And the benefits go way beyond that, as we discovered early in our own company's trajectory.

When we first founded Hugo, our software was focused solely on improving meeting preparation. To better understand the challenges our customers faced, we spent a lot of time in the field talking to people. We wanted to know everything that we could about what their experience was in Hugo so we could make it better. There were weeks when our founders spent more time outside the office, talking to customers, then inside doing the work.

The problem with this was that every conversation needed to be translated back into instructions and ideas for the rest of the team. Often, the team drew different conclusions than the founders from the same information. The system was inefficient, so, to increase our tempo, we decided to hack together a Slack plug-in to make it easier to quickly share customer meeting notes with engineering and design, in real time. The plugin-in was connected to our calendars so that it could automatically remind us to do this just after every meeting.

The impact was immediately apparent. It was suddenly as if the whole team was in the room hearing customer feedback — while they were doing their work in the office. It was so transformative to our business, that we realized we were solving a much more important problem than just meeting preparation. What happens after the meeting was just as impactful to our business, if not more so.

The Hugo that we are today is largely based on the enormous success of this simple activity. And it is still our practice to publish meeting notes in a public Slack channel. This goes for both team meetings where decisions are made, as well as other meetings, like when we speak to a potential partner about a marketing opportunity.

It only takes a few seconds for someone to read bullet point summaries of what happened in a meeting, but the upside of that kind of information sharing is huge.

Atlassian is built around a similar open culture, where sharing is the norm. "When I see people freaking out about an announcement or something, it often seems they're just freaked out that they didn't find out about it earlier," says Penny, a senior engineering manager, as she describes Atlassian's culture of proactive sharing. "I feel like a solution to that is more openness, rather than less."

Finding the right balance between what to share and what to hold back can be tricky, especially as an organization scales. This is going to look different for every organization, but it's a capability that is very worth exploring and cultivating.

Here's a quick framework to run through when deciding when to share and when not to. Ask yourself these questions:

- Does this information have the potential to positively influence others' work?
- Is this information to share, or simply information to capture?
- Is it need-to-know, nice-to-know, or distracting?
- Is this information timely, relevant, and accurate?
- Do I have consent to share this information?

How you make use of these questions is going to vary depending on your communication stack.

On our team, for example, we use Slack for everything urgent. Emails are typically only for information that is operating on a longer timeframe. We use Hugo for meeting notes. And we record videos as a fill-in for face-to-face conversations between a distributed team. Your team probably has its own micro-culture around how each of these channels are used.

In your unique communication stack, there are probably blind spots. If somebody isn't on an email chain or in a Slack room, are they missing out on specific information? If somebody doesn't attend a meeting, how will they gain access to what is shared? Deciding what and when to share is sometimes a function of eliminating these gaps.

To be effective, share information where employees already are. For example, 3M has employees distributed across 150 locations. Many are scientists working on new technologies. Their inboxes receive hundreds of new emails every day. It's easy for communications to get lost. So they use digital signage — screens placed at important places in their offices such as eating areas and reception desks — as part of their internal communication strategy. This may seem extreme for many teams (Slack works just fine for us), but it paints a good visual picture that you can emulate.

One word of caution about the 3M technique, though: It does nothing to foster two-way dialogue. Information sharing isn't a one-to-many interaction. Authentic communication is back-and-forth. There must be feedback loops. When everyone feels heard and responded to, trust and positive relationships across your team blossom.

Proactive sharing also requires being honest about when you choose not to share information that you should have. You are building a culture where everyone is going to be deeply committed to each other and a company's vision. So, instead of shielding people from information that might be seen as controversial, be honest with them and allow them to see and feel what it means to be alongside you.

In that vein, here are three questions you should ask yourself before your next team-wide or all-hands meeting (basically any meeting with six or more attendees).

1. What am I trying to protect my team from?
2. What am I not sharing as a result?
3. What is the impact on me, the team, and the company of withholding this information?

It's natural to want to withhold information. Instead, we suggest you allow yourself to be honest, authentic, and transparent about your concerns and struggles. It will help your people feel more connected and more invested in your company.

As you can see, proactive sharing increases the amount of information any given team member has access to — good, neutral, and bad. Armed with this information, you and your team can observe more of what is happening in your business and make smarter decisions.

"Observe" is also the first step in the OODA Loop, a process you use thousands of times a day, whether you know it or not. That's why it is so important to understand what the OODA Loop is, and how to make it work to your advantage.

---

1. Geckoboard (2015). Research Report: 'Mushroom Management' Leaves Employees Heading for the Door. Retrieved from www.geckoboard.com/learn/guides/mushroom-management/

6

INCREASE YOUR OODA
LOOP TEMPO

JOHN BOYD IS CONSIDERED to be the greatest U.S. fighter pilot to have ever lived. In simulated air-to-air combat, he once defeated every challenger in under forty seconds. His manuals of fighter tactics changed the way every air force in the world flies and fights.

Boyd noted that when engaged in a dogfight, a fighter pilot must work fast and juggle lots of decisions in real time. They are flying through the air at extreme speeds and tracking multiple moving objects in all directions. The tiniest error could mean certain death.

Dogfighting is more analogous to your own work than you might realize — minus the "certain death" part I hope. A pilot in their cockpit must worry about everything in three-dimensional space. Similarly, business exists in a multidimensional environment in which threats and opportunities can present themselves at any moment and from any direction.

In the face of the ambiguity and uncertainty surrounding us, it can be tempting to turn our gaze inwards, actively steering clear of the unknowable. Boyd disagrees with this tactic. He holds that rather than avoiding the unknown, you should *optimize* for it. He says that in the "fundamental and all-pervasive presence of uncertainty . . . action and decision become critically important."

At Hugo, we have learned from John's philosophies how to make decisions in extreme and uncertain situations. Boyd argued that our inability to make sense of our changing reality is our biggest hindrance. When circumstances change, we often fail to shift our perspective because it is in our nature to try to see the world *as we feel it should be.*

When encountering new problems, individuals and organizations often default to familiar mental models that have worked in the past to solve them. Should these mental models fail, it's human nature to keep trying to make them work. Charlie Munger, perhaps the world's wittiest billionaire, described this tendency as "Man with a Hammer syndrome" where "everything is a nail."

OODA Loop practices in action

Boyd's experience as a fighter pilot taught him that mental agility was the key to overcoming uncertainty. Based on his experience fighting against the more maneuverable Russian MiGs, he spent his entire life trying to understand this uncertainty and how to overcome it, resulting in a powerful framework called the OODA loop. Over time, experts have come to use his philosophy for much more than dogfights. It applies as much to actions in business as it does to military operations.

OODA stands for:

1. Observe
2. Orient
3. Decide
4. Act

Sounds simple, right? Think before you act. You probably already do this constantly. So why is the OODA loop such a game changer?

Because you're probably doing it wrong.

Observe

Everybody observes, every day. You might think that you're already quite good at it. But that's exactly that kind of complacency that Boyd warns against.

Let's look at a deliberately simple example. Suppose someone sent you the following text: "I'm sorry. I didn't realize you are an expert." There are a lot of ways to interpret that.

You have incomplete information, and your experiences will be based on your own filters. Now imagine you were talking to somebody on the phone, and they said the same thing very sarcastically. You realize that they are taking a jab at you, and you might react negatively. Or perhaps they say it in a face-to-face conversation, in the same sarcastic tone, but with a smile and a wink. In that context, their comment about you is lighthearted sarcasm — not an attack, but rather a signal of intimacy and confidence in your relationship.

Observing imperfect or incomplete information isn't the only problem. You can also perceive so much information that it becomes difficult to separate what is meaningful from what is not. Remember those old *Where's Waldo* books[1]? They contained page after page of large-format illustrations filled with comical scenes, ones that were packed with characters who resembled our hero and his signature red and white striped shirt and matching cap. Today's information-dense world can sometimes seem a lot like the puzzles from those pages. It becomes difficult to discern what's important from what isn't, especially at a glance.

For both of these reasons, when you observe, you must take into account not only your point of view, but also the density of new information about how the environment is changing. Rather than being closed off and defaulting to old mental models and assumptions, strive to be open, looking at circumstances anew.

When your mind is an open system, not a closed one, you are able to form new mental models and overcome confusion-inducing uncertainty. In the case of the above, you're likely to have a knee-jerk response to the sarcasm. But simply acknowledging what you know might be critical to reading the situation — and could even save a friendship.

In business, just as in war and life itself, you and your team must constantly grapple with unclear, changing, and challenging circumstances that are much more difficult than a simple text message. When things get tough, people tend to shut down. Our grand plans get confused and jumbled and we return to old habits.

In this state, denial (refusing to accept reality) and emotional filtering (wishing that reality was not happening) often take place. Both reactions prevent us from responding until they are overcome. Just being aware that we may be tempted to deny or filter information is often enough to help us overcome these reactions.

Luckily, the stakes for your team are not life-or-death. But having too little or too much information, plus denial, emotional filtering, and fatigue all play a role in your ability to observe the situation clearly.

Having the best information isn't enough to solve your problems, though. You're also going to need good judgement. That brings us to the next step: Orient.

Orient

Before you make a decision, orient your thinking. Clarify how you are interpreting what you are observing. While the observation step focuses on the external, orientation demands we look inward. Is there anything, internal to you, that is shaping your perceptions? Where are your biases? What assumptions need to be checked?

The orient stage is critical, but it's also hard, because you may be biased in ways you don't realize. Once you've analyzed your problem, you're most likely tempted to immediately start solving it. But if you do so without reviewing your biases first, you're putting yourself at a disadvantage.

Amy Edmondson, Novartis Professor of Leadership and Management at Harvard Business School, describes this as "the basic human challenge." In its simplest form, the challenge is that *it's hard to learn if you already know*. Edmondson says that to overcome this, we must be open to being curious.

Boyd presents the same idea. Challenge your mental models. Take apart old paradigms and put the pieces back together to create a new perspective that is more attuned to your current reality.

Doing this can feel odd — unsafe, even — if it's your first time. Thinking through problems is something we all do naturally every day. We just usually don't contemplate *how* we are going to think. We just *do it*. But that's exactly the point.

In our organization, we lean on a simple rule of involving team-wide or group-wide sharing and input to help strip out mental biases. We can do this because we operate as an idea meritocracy, where the best ideas always win — no matter who they come from. Team input also makes the next OODA phase, decision-making, easier to handle.

Digging more into our specific process, everything that arises from customer conversations related to our software is mapped to a specific board in Trello. This means that everyone can see the rationale behind upcoming product work. We go through these candidates weekly, in a forum where people can raise different points of view and suggest new ways of solving problems. In this way, Trello helps us achieve transparency and inclusiveness. Anyone can contribute to our sprint candidates, and everyone receives a Slack notification when changes are made to our Trello board.

As you can see, the OODA loop doesn't have to be a solo endeavor. Just as your team will often be involved in helping you orient, they will also participate in making a decision.

Decide

During your orientation phase, you and your team are going to come up with multiple alternatives on how to proceed. The decision step is where you pick one of those. It's important here not to get stuck in analysis paralysis. We found in our organization that rapid decision-making — call it tempo — is a tremendous advantage.

But how do you decide if you disagree as a team? Amazon CEO Jeff Bezos championed a solution in a 2016 shareholder letter where he coined the now-famous phrase "disagree and commit." He wrote:

> This phrase will save a lot of time. If you have conviction on a particular direction even though there's no consensus, it's helpful to say, "Look, I know we disagree on this but will you gamble with me on it? Disagree and commit?" By the time you're at this point, no one can know the answer for sure, and you'll probably get a quick yes.

In the letter, Bezos gave an example of his own use of the concept. When his team presented an Amazon Studios original for approval, he didn't want to move forward with it. It didn't seem interesting to him, it was a complex production, and the terms were not great.

But his team differed in opinion, so he immediately replied with "I disagree and commit and hope it becomes the most watched thing we've ever made." The result? A fast decision cycle and an immediate opportunity to get feedback on whether the decision was right. Think about how long it would have taken the team to convince Bezos he was wrong.

The alternative to disagreeing is for each point of view to continually concede until a consensus is reached. This can be dangerous. In our view, consensus on a bunch of great ideas can often result in one lackluster one. Sometimes it's better to commit to a single decision that has a real point of view and logic behind it than to water things down. Say we're choosing a logo color. I want blue, you want green, others want red, purple, white, and orange. A consensus choice might be to mix all of those together, resulting in a hideous gray-brown that satisfies no one. It would be better to take a chance on any one of the more pleasant-looking colors.

And who knows, no matter how well-reasoned your idea is, maybe someone else's decision will work just as well or better. It's impossible to perfectly predict what the outcome is going to be. That's why Boyd describes the Decide step as a hypothesis. We often have imperfect information, but we still need to move forward with our best educated guess. Every good hypothesis needs to be tested, which brings us to our final step.

Act

The OODA loop isn't just a decision-making process. It's a learning system. By using it, we all become scientists who perpetually test new hypotheses in the real world. The action step is how we determine whether our hypotheses are correct. It's easy to get intoxicated with a decision and rush to execute, missing this crucial aspect. Action is testing. Like any good scientist performing an experiment, you must observe and review your results. Thus begins the next cycle of the OODA Loop.

OODA is *always-on*. The word "loop" reminds us to be constantly improving how we operate. The real power of the loop happens when you keep running it, again and again and again — responding to new information generated by each previous loop. Whenever you observe something is less effective, you orient to different mental concepts, decide which ones to use, and then quickly act to test them out.

As you can see, the OODA loop makes our implicit decision-making process *explicit*. It works because it is a mental model that encompasses comfort with uncertainty, speed, embracing unpredictability, and rigorous testing — a perfect combination for facing a complex world head-on, iterating one step at a time. As such, it allows any person or team to better manage how they make decisions — and to make continuously better ones.

You'll find that many of the tips in this book will set up your team for running the OODA loop across all kinds of work streams, big and small. Here are a few we've already talked about:

- Establish a meeting cadence that brings everyone together. Meeting frequency should strike the right balance between new information and considering corrective action.
- Use a shared decision log to compare past decisions with their outcomes and to share these learnings with the team to increase the accuracy of future loops.
- Plan for alignment while conducting experiments. Build loops into your process so that you can easily adjust course and avoid stagnation.

Many of these activities are personally and emotionally complicated. To be successful, you and your team must have mutual trust. You're going to need to embrace vulnerability and have courage.

Bad decisions are a fact of life. Even when empowered by an efficient OODA loop, we're still bound to pursue ideas that turn out to be wrong. But often, being wrong turns out to be a blessing in disguise.

---

1. *Where's Waldo?* is the U.S. title. The books were originally a british series published under the moniker of *Where's Wally?*

7

CREATE A CULTURE WHERE
FAILURE ISN'T PUNISHED

ALL EXPERIMENTS HAVE AN OBJECTIVE, a hypothesis, and a result. After predicting an outcome and then seeing what happens, the next step is evaluation, which forms the basis for the next experiment. That is adaptability in a nutshell.

Intrinsically related to doing this successfully, however, is building a culture where it is okay to be wrong.

Cunningham's Law humorously states that "the best way to get the right answer on the internet is not to ask a question; it's to post the wrong answer." It's funny because it's *true*. But the internet isn't the only place where being wrong can be the fastest path to being right; just being wrong in general can be a great way to learn. You can only make use of this principle, though, if your culture doesn't punish well-meaning failure[1].

When you're a little bit right, there isn't very much to motivate you to do better. Average results are often expected. *Moving on . . .* But from a learning perspective, it's actually much better to experience lackluster results. The pain demands introspection. The sting of failure invites new ideas. What went wrong? What do we need to change? In the face of average results, you will almost never ask these important questions. And that's a loss.

As you increase your adaptability, connectedness, and tempo, you will be wrong — probably wrong more often. Embrace it. Revel in it. Do not allow errors to fill you with self-doubt and to hamper your momentum. They are the best way to accelerate your learning. Thank the failure for what it taught you, brush yourself off, and get up and try again.

You can teach your team to do the same thing. As a group, when your culture embraces failure, your team will be more willing to make mistakes that lead to even higher outcomes. The last thing that you want is everyone to play everything safe. You'll never get anywhere.

We talk a lot at Hugo about how we are going to 100X the company. It's not possible to do so without taking risks. And it's not possible to take risks without sometimes failing.

So be clear with your team on this one. Say it out loud: "We are going to do this thing, acknowledging that it may not work out exactly as we planned, but that's okay. We will learn more from our failures than from our successes."

Here are a few other tips to be more experimental and adaptable, and to help you embrace the possibility of failure:

1. Reframe the idea of failure as learning — *things we now know not to be true*. When referencing what hasn't worked in the past, cite it as something you have learned, not something that went poorly.
2. It's okay — and sometimes ideal — for takeaways from a team discussion to be a series of questions. Always concluding with decisions and solutions can be limiting.
3. Implement a place to track experiments. By declaring some decisions to be experiments, you are already leaving room for the possibility that they might be incorrect. Putting them all in one place will help you use the results

to reset objectives and come up with new ideas. A shared decision log is a great place to start.

---

1. Certainly if failure is the result of intentionally sloppy, misguided, or self-serving work, that's a different matter.

8

USE VULNERABILITY AS A TEAM-BUILDING SUPERCHARGER

"THIS WAS PROBABLY one of the worst decisions I've ever made." Josh smiled as he presented during our weekly all-hands meeting. "It turned out to be completely wrong." This is how Josh opened our decision log review a couple weeks ago. He could've done a lot to sweep his bad decision under the rug. Instead, he reveled in it. In fact, by starting with a terrible idea, we ended up with some pretty good information.

Yet it's not very common for the CEO and cofounder of a company to get up in front of everybody and say, "Not only was I completely wrong, but I'm happier for it," which is too bad. What this does is it normalizes being wrong. If the CEO can be wrong, then anybody can.

It's common for leaders to march on without acknowledging setbacks. There's a strong misperception that to be vulnerable might undermine authority. But in today's networked workplaces that are both open and connected, the opposite is true: Vulnerability increases authority. It demonstrates the willingness and courage to show up and be seen, despite uncertain outcomes.

You can't really innovate without the potential for risk and uncertainty. "If you've created a work culture where vulnerability isn't okay, you've also created a culture where innovation and creativity aren't okay," says Brené Brown, a research professor and bestselling author.

According to Brené's research, all transformational leaders have one thing in common: the capacity for difficult conversations. If you're going to risk being vulnerable, "you're going to get your ass kicked," says Brené. In this way, resilience, courage, and vulnerability are intertwined.

Teaching vulnerability to your team isn't always going to be easy, but it is achievable. Here are a few practical ways to get it started.

Lead by example

It often falls on the leaders in an organization to model this kind of behavior. In doing so, they demonstrate through action that the company values vulnerability and boldness. So just as you want to build a culture that doesn't punish failure, embrace the flip side of that equation. You're going to need to ask for help sometimes. You don't have to do everything yourself. Be authentic, caring, and vulnerable. This makes people comfortable with you, which in turn will help them open up.

Treat missteps with warmth

Nobody likes to make mistakes. They can cause pain, disappointment, and even sadness. Screwing up takes the wind out of our sails. Being vulnerable doesn't change that. But you can change how failures serve you and your team. Brown says, "The goal is not to close yourself off from ever feeling pain. That's how you lose your capacity to take it all in."

Emphasize innovation

Your team is only going to be able to have original, creative ideas by being authentic. This naturally requires vulnerability. If you emphasize doing the same thing that you've always done, you are also discouraging innovation. On this point, Brown says, "Your level of vulnerability completely predicts the originality of your work."

Make a daily commitment to vulnerability

The more you practice being vulnerable, the better you will become at it. Vulnerability is a muscle that can be trained. At first you may feel exposed and uncomfortable. But when you make it a habit to expose yourself, after a while, you won't even feel vulnerable any longer. You'll just be open and authentic.

In this section, we've looked at myriad tools and techniques to help you make more effective decisions in your organization. A strong culture is built around faster and better decision-making, where all team members are able to make unique and useful contributions.

Developing a positive culture around decision-making is just one of many parts leaders play in supporting a 10X Culture. In the next section, we'll look at other things leaders can do to empower their team.

SUMMARY: 10X DECISION-MAKING

- Decision-making is a foundation of team culture and an invaluable focus because it impacts how all work gets done.
- Teams make better decisions when there is a shared consciousness — created through developing mutual trust, serving a common purpose, and sharing knowledge.
- Implementing a shared decision log will improve your tempo, increase worker autonomy, and eliminate hindsight bias.
- Use the OODA Loop to remove biases and make better decisions, faster.
- Approach challenges as opportunities to learn by embracing the possibility of failure as part of your team culture.
- Be vulnerable to demonstrate a willingness to show up and be seen, improve team cohesion, and empower your organization.

III

10X LEADERSHIP

Humans are social animals. Much of the culture in a team is a group effort. It is the sum of the actions and values of every team member, as they are exhibited every day. For better or worse, however, leaders have a disproportionate ability to impact a team's culture.

"Do as I say, not as I do" doesn't work for modern teams. Leaders must lead by example. When they do, they signal to everyone around them that striving for a team-oriented culture is not just a talking point, and is a worthy goal. It is something that has management buy-in.

That's why an entire section of this book is dedicated to leadership. People at any level in an organization will benefit from the content here — it's not all for the C-suite. To motivate your peers, to exert influence and to achieve the business outcomes you're striving for is a function of leadership.

If you're going to help lead your company to a 10X Culture, recognize that change can take time, but that's no reason to give up. This section contains a few secrets to help you along the way.

9

USE THE LANGUAGE TO SHAPE REALITIES

In a TED Talk presented in November 2017, cognitive scientist Lera Boroditsky demonstrated that how we use language shapes the way we think.

To illustrate this, she drew on examples from an Aboriginal group who have no word for right or left. She examined the Russian language, where there are multiple words for light blue (*goluboy*) and dark blue (*siniy*). In many languages, there are even grammatical genders — the sky in French is *le ciel* ("le" indicating that the sky is male).

In studying the people who use these languages, Boroditsky demonstrated that language and words profoundly shape the way we think about complex, impactful concepts such as:

- Space and time
- Decision-making
- Blame and punishment

All of this is due to the plasticity of the human mind. "The language that you speak shapes the way you think," says Boroditsky.

"That gives you the opportunity to ask, 'Why do I think the way I do? How could I think differently?' And also, 'What thoughts do I wish to create?'"

Could building a 10X Culture be as simple as changing how you speak? It is certainly a good start, especially for the leaders in an organization — because language doesn't just influence your reality, it impacts everyone around you.

It's not uncommon in a workplace to hear that someone must *deal* with a customer. This frames the customer as a problem. Simply changing that word to *assist* — or another similarly positive expression — changes how you think of customers, and by extension how customers are treated.

The big box store Target does something similar. Instead of calling their shoppers *customers*, Target refers to them as *guests*[1]. Again, this changes interactions from purely transactional to kind and friendly, which has yielded outstanding results for Target's reputation.

Language doesn't just shape customer service, though; it also shapes how you view and treat your team at work. For example, you can choose to refer to people within your organization as *employees, coworkers, team members*, or, like we do at Hugo, *thought partners*. Each offers a slightly different subtext that leads to different actions and different results.

Word choice is just one aspect of shaping your team's environment through language. There's also an entire communication framework that you can employ: *the language of leadership*.

The language of leadership

Effective leaders communicate differently. When you speak in this *leadership language,* you can more easily create a vision that inspires action and engages your team. Here are the building blocks of that language.

Clarity

The primary, non-negotiable tip in using the language of leadership is to strive for clarity. It doesn't matter what you're saying if nobody is receiving the message. This means that you need to choose your words carefully. Overly complex ideas or expressions can easily lose your audience. Leading is not an opportunity to look smart, but rather a function where you must use clear, simple language that conveys your intended meaning.

Brevity

Similarly, the language of leadership is concise. Get to the point. Everyone on your team is likely already inundated with information. So it's important that when you deliver yours, it's delivered in a way such that it doesn't get lost in the mix. Don't ramble or go off on tangents, or you risk losing your audience. Put the most important ideas at the beginning, and summarize them at the end.

Storytelling

Effective leaders use storytelling in their communication. You may have noticed that throughout this book, there are imaginative, evocative stories. Months from now, when you think back to having read this, you'll probably remember those stories more than sections like this one that are composed mostly of helpful, actionable tips.

Humans love stories. When we hear them, we produce elevated levels of the feel-good hormone oxytocin, which is linked to feelings such as trust, compassion, and empathy. "We are, as a species, addicted to stories. Even when the body goes to sleep, the mind stays up all night, telling itself stories," says Jonathan Gottschall, author of *The Storytelling Animal: How Stories Make Us Human*. So paint a picture when you're speaking. Insert relevant examples to retain the attention of your audience and help them remember your words.

Empathy

When leaders speak, they are also constantly listening and perceiving their audience's reaction. Keep the emotional dynamics of the room on your radar. Don't just focus on yourself, but be in tune with how your words are being received. Leverage your emotional intelligence. Read and respond to the room.

There's often an opportunity to adapt your message based on the reactions you're getting. The most capable leaders I know are constantly doing this on the fly. As you do, you may find that there are other voices that are waiting to be heard. Be respectful. Don't dominate the conversation — even if it's *your* conversation. Allow other voices to speak, and engage with them.

Decisiveness

Leaders speak using action-oriented terms. It's not enough just to be idealistic. You need to be clear and concrete about things that have happened, are underway, and are planned for the future. Position your strategies and ideas in reality. This will help connect your team and the activities that they are engaging in with the broader vision you're trying to convey.

THE LANGUAGE of leadership isn't a skill that you learn and then never need to return to again. Like most skills worth cultivating, it's an ongoing effort. It's also an introspective one. So how do you know when you're communicating effectively as a leader, and where you need to work on improving? Here are three specific tips.

Record your meetings. It's so easy with products like Zoom to record your meetings in the cloud. Click that button — and of course announce to everyone on the call that you are recording. You will learn a lot reviewing critical parts of meetings when you listen to your own language.

Just as professional athletes and video game players review their game footage daily and weekly to look for areas to improve, you too can watch how your team reacts and responds to the different language that you use. The first time you do this, it will be uncomfortable. But in time, this discomfort will give way to a motivation to improve.

Measure your LNPS. Much like the NPS that we seek from our customers, Employee Net Promoter Score (eNPS) is a measure of employee engagement that asks, "On a scale of 0 to 10, how likely is it that you would recommend this company as a place to work?"

But that's a company-level question. You or your HR team can make this more specific by performing an LNPS which is focused on specific leaders and managers. Tweak the question to say, "On a scale of 0 to 10, how likely would you recommend working for [insert name]?" This is a quick health check to get a reading of your teams' feelings toward you as a leader, which can be a great catalyst for conversation to continuously improve.

Hold one-on-ones. Consider covering language in your one-on-one template. Regularly ask your reports for feedback on your language and communication with questions such as, "Can you think of a time where I could've said something in a better way?" or "How did you feel about [insert meeting or discussion]?"

WHETHER YOU'RE A LEADER, manager, or otherwise, how you use language is important. Not only does it impact all of our communications, but it shapes our worldviews. Here's one last place to begin changing how you use language in your own life and work. You just need to eliminate a single word from your vocabulary.

Should.

Should is indecisive. When you say you *should* do something, it's more like a wish than an action. Do you actually do the things you say you "should do?" It is better to commit. If you end a meeting saying,

"We should make the following changes," have you really decided anything? Your action item lacks conviction.

Should is also negative, because it implies that something isn't already happening. Should is wishful thinking that denies reality.

But what if reality is coming at you full force? Boyd's OODA Loop shows us how uncertain, unknown challenges are popping up everywhere. In our connected, modern world, uncertainty is the status quo. As a leader, where do you go from here?

Well, you're going to have to figure out something quick. Sounds like it is time to improvise.

———————————————

1. Using the term "guests" outside the hospitality industry was first adopted by Disney in the 1950s to refer to people who visited their theme parks.

10

PRACTICE IMPROVISATIONAL LEADERSHIP

IN THE COMEDY improv show *Whose Line Is It Anyway?*, guests have to act out wacky scenes with little-to-no time to prepare. Somehow, their jokes and sketches are always interesting, funny, and original — and they deliver this kind of comedy over and over again.

Just as this type of improv requires performers to be nimble, creative, and ready to adapt without notice, today's leaders must respond in real-time as circumstances shift around them.

In the old model of management, sometimes referred to as the *bureaucratic model*, leadership focused heavily on research, planning, and control. Because embracing openness and autonomy in your workplace turns those principles around, it also requires new strategies for leadership — the *improvisational model* — which, like the OODA Loop, is a helpful tool for triumphing in our constantly evolving and uncertain future.

Drawing on research from psychology and neuroscience, Malcolm Gladwell's book *Blink: The Power of Thinking Without Thinking* argues that you don't need to process heaps of data or engage in endless introspection to make a good decision. You can make difficult choices in the blink of an eye. Gladwell claims that snap decisions made on instinct are usually more reliable than decisions based on careful planning and research.

What is it called when you make snap decisions based on incomplete knowledge? That's *improvisation.*

Frank J. Barrett, who is both a professor at the Naval Postgraduate School in Monterey and a professional jazz pianist, explains that improvisation is a vital precursor to innovation: "To be innovative, managers — like jazz musicians — must interpret vague cues, face unstructured tasks, process incomplete knowledge, and yet they must take action anyway."

As a leader of an innovative team, what are some core improv skills that you can apply in your daily work?

Heighten your perceptions

The nature of improv is that all of the inputs for the scenario are being given to you on the spot. Whereas normally you might witness meetings, participate in email and chat conversations, review planning documents, and then iterate over a period of time, improv condenses all of that context into the single moment of the present.

That's why the best improvisational leaders are able to heighten their perception — especially their listening skills — when they're in these situations. They recognize that in order to be able to react well and make the right decisions, they need to drink as much as they can from the firehose right then.

We've all heard ad infinitum that listening is a core skill in business and in your personal relationships. Despite knowing that's true, it can be difficult to remember to listen actively, especially when you have something to say. In those moments when you realize you are waiting to express yourself, pay attention to whether you're listening to your own voice inside your head, or to what other people are saying. You might be surprised at how often you're paying more attention to yourself than to those around you.

Then take that a step further. Are there other senses you're not making use of that could enhance your perception and enable you to improvise better?

Take risks and seek disruption

In improv, there's no doing things the same way they've always been done. It's got to be new and fresh every time. So the entire thing is always a risk. That tension is part of what makes it so entertaining.

Well, work can be fun, too, when leaders introduce incremental disruption to their teams. Encourage people to leap out of their comfort zones. The more you innovate, and the more you are willing to take risks — even small ones — the stronger your teams' cultural muscles will be for the risks that matter.

When something isn't working, actors often have to change things up on the fly. In doing so, you learn that change is just another part of the process toward getting it right.

In Frank Barrett's book *Yes to the Mess: Surprising Leadership Lessons from Jazz,* he tells a story of Miles Davis's improvisational technique. Miles was known to call out a song for his band to begin playing; but he would change the key they started in each time, so the band was forced to adapt.

A similar practice can help make your organization naturally adaptable — a critical feature of successful businesses. Your need to adapt is inevitable, so why not be good at it when the stakes are lower?

The trick here is to encourage — and perhaps go so far as to create — disruption on your teams, so your improv skill set isn't only being developed when you are under duress.

Yes, and...

Barrett says, "We are at our best when we're open to the world. Effective improvisation is born out of an attitude of radical receptivity — saying 'yes' to whatever situation is handed to you." Even in improv theater, it's well known that you should not say "no" to or disagree with your stage partner.

Never saying "no" to an idea is a pretty established concept. It's easy, though, to fall into a worse trap: the deadly "yes, but...." That simple phrase deprecates and redirects the ideas of others. In improv and in business, this kind of negativity demoralizes and demotivates. Often, "yes, but" comes as the result of our personal inhibition and risk aversion getting in the way.

Instead, just go for it! Try "yes, and..." When you do, you invite open communication by building upon the other person's ideas. It's an easy way to create a culture of acceptance. This is another example of using language to shape your reality. It may seem trivial. But even one or two words can be the difference between squashing a great conversation dead in its tracks and successfully creating something entirely new.

Learn to lead — and to follow

When an improv troupe is on stage, each person's roles must change and adapt seamlessly. The person who is leading one moment is following the next. Leadership has a similar ebb and flow. Sometimes you must lead with vision and goals. Other times you follow the ideas and innovations of others. You learn when to lead, when to follow, and how to do both at the same time.

Everything's an offer

Robert Poynton, author of *Everything's an Offer*, takes a unique view on how to improvise as a leader. He says that to an improviser, an offer is anything and everything you can take and use, including errors, mistakes, shortcomings, or absences.

When something unexpected occurs — often with my team, customers, partners, or investors — I try to construe the new information I have as an offer. How can I take and use what's just happened as an opportunity? The situation remains the same, but the improv mindset will help you approach setbacks differently.

You may be thinking that this focus on leader improv is inconsistent with some of the earlier advice on planning. Poynton disagrees: "Without the ability to adapt and flex, the best plan in the world will crash as soon as it meets reality. The problem is that we do a lot to develop our planning skills, and little or nothing to develop our improvisational skills."

You are partially right, though. Improvisation isn't applicable 100 percent of the time. While it might be effective as a project kicks off or a challenge unfolds, suddenly changing direction as you approach the end of your planning can have a randomizing effect.

As you can see, improvisational leadership can help foster collaboration and innovation. It impacts the energy and attitude of everyone at the workplace, potentially improving team discussions and communication in general. Cultivating improvisational skills will help you react and adapt more seamlessly. Using improvisation, you can set a positive example that will energize your team.

11

REFRAME MANAGERS AS COACHES
AND CULTURAL GUARDIANS

As a dance troupe leader and former yoga instructor, Brittany has the calm and easy demeanor of someone who is a pro at relaxing and going with the flow. Yet she's the type of individual you might call *Type A* — a relentless blend of hustle and empathy.

"So, tell me where you're blocked." That was how she opened every one-on-one with me. It was my first job at a tech startup, and I was still not used to the framing of these conversations. At every job I'd had before, meetings like this were all about the status of my projects — where I was at and what my next steps were.

But with Brittany, there were no mandated status updates. We had already decided on my priorities. It was up to me to figure out how to execute. In these conversations, Brittany made it clear to me that as my boss, she saw it as her primary job to remove obstacles that prevented me from doing my work. If I wanted her help, all I had to do was ask.

As my career has unfolded and I've found myself managing others, I've always strived to be this kind of mentor — more of a coach than a taskmaster. You should do this too, even though something inside you will resist it.

Why? Managing as a coach is a radical departure from our traditional view of management. This old view has been deeply rooted in command and control, and in many ways resembles the dynamic between parent and child, not between team members. This parent/child relationship that defines many manager relationships has its roots in the industrial revolution. It's built on assumptions which, for most workers, no longer apply.

Those assumptions can be traced back in large part to the work of one man: Frederick W. Taylor. The son of a hard-working lawyer, Taylor nearly permanently damaged his eyesight from assiduous studying in the dim light of night. His passion was taken by the inner workings of mechanical shops and manufacturing plans, and was the first to suggest that managers should be involved in two aspects of the business: planning and training. They should determine the one best way to accomplish any given task, and then hire the best people possible to perform that task.

Find a person of a suitable skill level, advised Taylor. Train them in a specific way. Pay them a fair wage — no more, no less. This strategy was called "scientific management," because it emphasizes improving worker productivity through scientific analysis. Taylor explored factors like the positions of machines on a manufacturing floor, the actions workers needed to perform, and the way they moved their bodies to perform these actions. He optimized *everything*.

Scientific management has its merits, and was successful in transforming industries in the early twentieth century. But now, more than 100 years after Taylor published *The Principles of Scientific Management*, the legacy of these practices remains in many industries that are far different than a manufacturing line.

There is no *one task* anymore. There is no verifiably perfect solution. Modern companies exist in a far more complex environment. Inputs and outputs aren't fixed and easily measured. Whereas there are precise, documentable steps that need to be taken to build a car, if you're in marketing, sales, product, engineering — just about any function other than manufacturing — you're operating in a world of uncertainty, where no one can know with absolute certainty the best way to perform a specific task.

As a leader, even if you can't know precisely how workers should complete their work, you still have to be able to support them. To do so, begin by shedding the conventions of scientific management. Instead, embrace a style of leadership that plays to the need for adaptable teams that exchange ideas openly in a trusting environment. To do that, leaders must shift from focusing on planning and training to being mentors and cultural guardians in their organizations.

For example, consider a manager whose direct report is working on an important project. The success of this project will be a reflection on both manager and employee. Now, the manager might be tempted to use scientific management — dictating all of the steps the employee must take to do the work, and rigorously monitoring her performance.

Instead, we propose a different approach: Try to help the employee learn and grow. It's one of the most rewarding experiences you can have as a manager. Here are some tips to help you get started.

Ask, don't tell

You probably have a lot of expertise you're dying to share. That's fine when you're clarifying action steps for projects or when people come to you asking for advice. But when operating as a coach, try to restrain your impulse to give answers.

Open-ended questions, not answers, are the essential tools of coaching. You must help your team member articulate their challenges and their goals, and then find their own answers. When the solution to a problem is their idea, your team member will be more committed to putting it into action.

Build accountability to commitments

Commitments cut both ways. As a leader and a coach, you're going to have to do what you say you're going to do. But it's also useful to build accountability on the employee side.

Accountability increases the likelihood of success. It improves the positive impact of a conversation because it solidifies the discussion into concrete ideas. So, if decisions are being made during your conversation, talk about deadlines. Be on the lookout for loose commitments — like if the word *should* starts to rear its ugly head.

One way to do this is with your tools. Turn action items into Asana tasks, Trello cards, and Jira issues. By locking tasks into the systems that you use every day at work, you're transforming *shoulds* into units of work that are going to get done.

12

PROVIDE OBJECTIVES, NOT PLANS

IN HIS LANDMARK management book *What Got You Here Won't Get You There*, Marshall Goldsmith points out an interesting trend in leadership. The higher you get in an organization, the more your suggestions become interpreted as orders. Merely being a leader makes it harder to empower others in your organization to contribute their best.

So how do you help guide and direct your company while still allowing people to feel ownership of their projects? Give them objectives to meet, not plans to execute.

We're not advocating providing objectives without giving input as to how they can be successfully achieved. Leading also involves contributing strategy, ideas, and resources so that team members can be successful. But always frame these conversations in terms of the objectives, where everything that comes after is a recommendation or resource.

This ties into another of Goldsmith's main points. In his book, he shines a bright light on a concept in leadership he refers to as *adding too much value*. By contributing too much to projects, you actually diminish others' ownership of their ideas. When you add to the idea, it no longer feels like it is their idea — which kills momentum. It also quickly devolves into micromanagement, which stifles creativity and suppresses employee potential.

Adding too much value also deprives your team members of gaining satisfaction from their work. Daniel Pink discusses this with his notion of autonomy in *Drive: The Surprising Truth About What Motivates Us*. According to Pink, autonomy motivates us to think creatively because we don't need to conform to strict rules. He suggests rethinking traditional ideas of control — up to and including regular office hours, dress codes, and (controversially) numerical goals — in order to increase staff autonomy and boost innovation, creativity, and engagement.

You can see how even if you think your plans and ideas are better, the ultimate outcome will often be worse if you deprive your team of autonomy. What's better is to identify new opportunities leading to the agreed outcome. Then trust each other to get the job done. To help you take this approach, whenever you are setting up a project, ask yourself the following questions.

Am I framing this in terms of the expected outcome, or what I think should be done?

Often, this requires taking the idea or proposed solution in your head, and zooming out to identify the objective. This can feel counterintuitive. As you take a step back, you feel like you're throwing away your great idea. But you're not. You're sharing what you really care about with the intelligent group around you, in case your conclusion isn't the best solution. Start with the results you're aiming for, and work your way down from there.

Working with product and engineering teams, this is easy to mess up. There's a strong temptation to take a solution to engineering and ask them to implement it. But more often than not, telling them what we're trying to achieve leads to a much better outcome. The engineers' fresh solution usually works better, solves other problems we didn't consider, and gets built quicker. And if what they come back with is dramatically different than what I was thinking, and doesn't look like it's going to work, then I can begin to ask questions about why they are approaching the problem in that way.

Is it clear that the suggestions I am making are in fact suggestions?

Framing things in terms of objectives doesn't mean that you can't contribute ideas. It means you need to provide suggestions, not marching orders. How do you do this? How do you make yourself a resource to help unblock team progress, rather than a dictator mapping out every step they take? It's a combination of mindset, culture, and careful word choice.

One technique that we like to use in design reviews at Hugo is to try to only ask questions. So instead of saying something like, "I think this button isn't prominent enough and that people are going to miss it," we might ask, "Do you think that users will be able to notice this button the way that it is currently styled?"

See how a simple reframing of a declarative sentence into a question immediately eliminates the idea that this might be an order? It is still an important point to take in, but it gives the designer an opportunity to receive feedback, think through the logic, and make a decision based on their own point of view and expertise. They may have had a good reason for the original design, which they now will share with you.

As Steve Jobs said, "It doesn't make sense to hire smart people and then tell them what to do. We hire smart people so they can tell us what to do."

To do this successfully, you need to deliberately take time out of your schedule to stop and orient yourself, because you're in charge. With the mutual trust that you've built up, your team is counting on you to make sure they're headed in the right direction.

13

VARY YOUR PERSPECTIVE

As we talked about earlier, we call our most important team meeting at Hugo a HiLo. It's short for high + low (Australians love to abbreviate things). We named the meeting this as a reminder to regularly look at the business from multiple vantage points. From high-level strategy to in-the-weeds detail, we take a look at our organization from a variety of perspectives.

The format of the HiLo emphasizes an important point in planning and perspective: Your long-range vision should influence your quarterly goals, which in turn influence your weekly goals, and so on. It goes the other way too. What you do on any given day impacts and is impacted by what you do in a week. What you do in a week impacts your orientation for a month.

Here are a few other techniques you can implement to ensure your perspective is properly varied.

Use a decaying plan

One strategy you may find useful in varying your perspective is to use a *decaying plan*. It's nowhere near as bad as it sounds.

When we're planning for twelve months, for example, the first ninety days is well-defined. We have clear ideas, tactics, and experiments figured out. We outline the resources required and the outcomes we're aiming for. Our six-month plan, though, is about half as detailed. We know where we are headed — that's necessary to continue where our ninety-day plan leaves off — but how we're going to get there isn't as clearly defined. It's a vision at a lower level of fidelity. Then our twelve-month plan and beyond is primarily simply vision and direction.

Even though Hugo is a product for businesses, as a freemium product that can be adopted by anyone, we have a steady flow of new users and new information. That means we are able to move very quickly compared to, for example, enterprise software that lands much fewer accounts in a year at higher price points. So for us, twelve months is an eternity.

Your team's equivalent may be two years, or even five years. Still, ask yourself: Does your organization's planning have the right level of fidelity for each time frame? If not, you could be at a disadvantage — either spending too much time over-planning, or putting yourself in a weak position for the future by under-planning.

Leverage the diversity of your team

The three authors of 10X Culture have widely different backgrounds. Darren was a lawyer, Josh comes from product management, and I (Rob) am a marketer. Everyone comes to every issue with a unique point of view and experience to back it up. Often, when the same question is posed to the three of us, there are three new and different perspectives to consider.

So varying your perspective isn't necessarily only a function of whether you're looking at things strategically, tactically, or in the details. It also has to do with whose perspective is being captured. Consider leveraging the roomful of perspectives that you have available to you more often.

Change your environment

Sometimes there's no better way to change your perspective than to look at the same situation from a different physical position. Get away. Go for a walk. Take the team outside. Suddenly, you'll see things very differently.

There's a psychological reason for this that has to do with habits and associations. When you remain in the same environment, you are primed to think the same way and revert to habits that you have practiced in that environment. But by shifting your body to something less familiar, you allow those habits to recede. The cues and contexts that normally influence your behavior are no longer present. Neither are your routines. This unlocks the brain and allows you to approach your thinking from a fresher perspective.

Understand that your perspective is limited

At times, you'll need to challenge the facts and premises that have created your situation. What is actually a fact, and what is a belief? When you start to break down what you truly know, and what you think you know, the answers may be right in front of you.

It can be helpful here to give your beliefs a confidence score. There are many things that aren't exactly facts but you are almost sure they are true. There are others where it's more your point of view and experience, but you don't really have sufficient evidence to declare that an idea is a fact, so to speak.

Treating an assumption as fact can be a zero-multiplier in any situation. Everything that follows is premised on that "fake fact." Acknowledge this and own it. If you don't question or challenge your beliefs, they can disrupt your entire thought process.

Perhaps the most important perspective of all is the customer. Legend has it that at Amazon, there's a rule that every meeting must have one empty chair. That chair embodies the customer. It serves as a constant reminder of the importance of looking at every decision from the customer's point of view. Is this good for our customers? Will it make them happy? Will it make things easier for them?

Your customers are the lifeblood of your business. Luckily, your company's 10X Culture will help you produce 10X customers in kind.

SUMMARY: 10X LEADERSHIP

- Careful use of language is shapes how you and your team think and feel. Eliminate problematic words that encourage negative behavior, and introduce positive ones.
- Hone your skills as an improvisational leader. Be in the moment, listen actively, take risks, say "yes," and learn when to lead and when to follow.
- Think of management as coaches and cultural guardians whose primary purpose is to make the team more effective. Always be looking out for ways to help your employees develop themselves into something greater.
- Empower team members by giving them goals and objectives. Don't outline every step along the way. Encourage autonomy by letting them own their problems while still helping to solve them.
- Regularly vary your perspective. By looking at issues from a variety of vantage points, angles, and points of view, you enable new and profound insights to emerge. Take more walks.

IV

---

10 X CUSTOMERS

Thus far, this book has been focused on the internal culture of your team, and specifically how to create a more open, adaptable, motivated group that maximizes the potential of every member. Stopping with an internal-only perspective on culture would be a bit naïve. After all, no business is totally independent. You have industry contacts and partners — and most importantly, you have customers.

In this section, we'll dig into how a company's culture is influenced by its customer relationships.

Your customers are your *raison d'être*. You can't use culture as a weapon to fight for growth in your organization if you ignore the part your customers play in it.

Remember Atlassian's provocative core value from the title of Chapter 1?

Don't f*#k the customer.

This was one of the first values that they decided on. And it comes up often. It's not uncommon to hear the phrase cited verbatim during a discussion at Atlassian: "Does this f*#k the customer?"

The language drives the point home. Your customers are not just a commodity that drives your numbers up; they are an extension of your team. Their success is critical for your success. This mental reframe is a subtle change, but it can lead to big outcomes.

Happy, dedicated, trusting customers offer amazing benefits for your business. On the home front, your customer-facing teams will feel more rewarded and motivated with every customer. Your customers will offer you insights and perspectives that will enhance your understanding of the market, and what they and other customers truly need. Plus, these customers are more likely to stay on in the long run and refer their networks to you.

So imagine your team culture helping to build an army of customers who are loyal and helpful to your company. You can do this by embracing many of the principles in this book to use in your customer interactions. When you truly start to look at customers as an extension of your own team, the potential is profound.

But customers have their own needs, desires, and motivations. At times, they may be antagonistic or demanding. They are not necessarily predisposed to building a supportive and thriving relationship with you. Many customers are altruistic, but that's not something that you can rely on. It is, however, something you can cultivate.

14

CUSTOMER INSIGHTS ARE NO LONGER NICE-TO-KNOW

LIKELY, only a portion of your team is customer-facing. In most companies, the majority of people in the business rarely talk to customers. Yet everyone on the team is responsible for keeping the business running — a pursuit that ultimately serves those customers.

That's why it is so critical to cultivate an understanding of your customers' needs, desires, and successes with your broader team. This is the kind of information that people need to power their OODA Loops (Observe, Orient, Decide, Act) and enable the best thinking as part of your idea meritocracy.

Plus, when you arm your entire team with true empathy for the customer they are helping, you make it easier for people to find purpose and enthusiasm for their work — another key cultural component.

Listen to your customers

Teams that talk to their customers generally build better products. They offer better services. Conversely, teams that lack an understanding of their customers will make mistakes. They might build the wrong software, or they might go after a portion of the market that isn't going to drive as much growth as they thought.

Early in my software career, I gave a presentation on my business to most of the engineering team at my company. Many had been coding the product for years. While they had a general understanding of the business, when you really dug down into it, most of them were ignorant of exactly how their company's software was being used and who was using it. They were getting detailed specs from the product team on what to build, but they lacked any real context as to *why*.

As a result, engineers were prioritizing the quality of certain features that provided little value to the customers and deprecating other areas that they didn't realize were important. The result was a software platform designed for enterprise use that had glaring quality gaps and was unsuitable for the marketplace. It took almost a year of fixing to get it ready.

To prevent your team from ending up in a similar situation, provide broad access to customer feedback and insights. Make sure everyone in your company can picture the customer in their mind and knows what makes your customers tick.

You need a way for your entire business to "hear" from your customers so that your team can do their best work every day and make decisions that truly represent the customer's interests. Our primary place for doing this is Slack. One channel we maintain is called "Customer Insights."

There, we post all of the notes from the meetings we have with customers. After reading a handful of bullet points, any team member can absorb the most important insights from those conversations – it's almost as if they were in the room. Some of our customers separate this out and have a channel for each customer segment, posting notes accordingly so people can focus on the insights that impact their team most.

Another Slack channel we use shows results from automated forms that we send out when certain criteria are met — such as when an organization using our software grows to a certain size. The surveys offer a small Amazon gift card as an incentive for completion, and they provide a way for us to automatically keep track of our customer base.

From the surveys, we don't just get a simple NPS score. We ask people how they are using Hugo, which teams have adopted it, and why they got started in the first place.

If you don't have something like this in place, consider adding it in your organization. For the cost of a handful of gift cards, you'll get invaluable insights, and the automation ensures you get a constant drip of feedback even when you don't have time to invest in reaching out.

In addition to sharing notes on meetings and surveys, it's also critical to expose the activities that happen as a result of your day-to-day operations. Successful onboarding, renewals, up-sells, survey results — so many customer data points are easy to share and celebrate.

Renewals start on day one

Having all of this visibility and noise around the customer keeps your team aligned on what matters most. It's *not* that software that they're building, or that content the marketing team is creating — those are means to an end. What matters most is the successful, growing, and loyal customer.

Keeping customers is a constant effort. Without the right perspective and team culture around customer success, it's easy to ignore customers if they aren't in a position to immediately churn. But waiting until the contract is up for renewal to re-engage a customer who has been drifting away is usually far too late; they've likely already made up their minds.

When to fire a customer

A useful aspect of investing in customer visibility within your company has to do with understanding who your best customers are — and which ones aren't a good fit. It's just as important to not be distracted by bad-fit customers as it is to stay focused on good-fit ones.

Many businesses follow the 80/20 rule, where roughly the top 20 percent of customers make up 80 percent of their revenue. But often, efforts and resources in sales, marketing, customer support, and product are poorly mapped to this distribution. In some cases, the most challenging customers are actually the least profitable.

In my time training and coaching sales teams, one of the hardest skills to teach has always been how to disqualify quickly. As uncomfortable as it may be to do, this should be a focus for most salespeople. It's better for everyone that you don't waste each other's time if the sale is never going to close.

This isn't just a problem in sales. For a freemium SaaS tool like Hugo, we get a lot of different people trying our software. Some want Hugo to solve a problem for them that we simply do not solve.

For example, we do not automatically transcribe meeting recordings. Rather than generate page after page of potentially error-ridden transcription, we've focused our app on being the most efficient way for a human to capture their own meeting insights. When it becomes clear that someone is really looking for transcription, we make our case. But if they're steadfast, rather than try to convince them to stay on a user, it's often better to help them move on.

Sometimes the most successful thing you can do with the customer is to show them that they will not be successful with you. The suggestion that you *fire* your customers, though, may be a little hyperbolic. Very rarely should you actually tell them they are no longer welcome to do business with you.

You can and should direct your resources, however, to your more profitable, pleasant customer segments. This includes efforts on the customer acquisition side, in marketing, product development, and customer support. By reallocating resources to where they are needed, you focus less on the customers that are a burden to you, helping them self-select out of being your customer. In the meantime, those better-fit customers are getting stronger signals from you — and hopefully growing.

Discerning whether a potential customer relationship is going to be successful is not always an easy task. On the quantitative side, you can mine your internal data and match what you know against profiles and personas about your different customers. But don't discount qualitative information, such as customer interviews in which your customers explain to you in their own words the value they get from your products and services.

That brings us to our next topic: seeking feedback from your customers, an activity that is critical to your overall culture of customer success. Being able to learn as much as you can from your customers, as well as act on that information, is crucial for your company.

15

THE CULTURE OF CUSTOMER TRADEOFFS

How you make decisions about your product with regard to your customer needs is a cultural challenge. It's a function that is rooted in your norms and values. And with finite resources and conflicting information, it's not always easy.

Companies guide their decisions using information from *a lot* of sources. Customer insights are invaluable, yes, but that doesn't capture the full picture of your business. Some customer information will be highly actionable. Some will be misguided. Some will be confusing — or just plain wrong.

So when you look at how you operate — strategies such as how to build your product or staff your services — it falls on you to make the right tradeoffs for both your organization and the customer. This can be tough because it sometimes means saying no when you want to say yes. It can also require humility and admitting that a customer understands your business better than you do.

Further, one customer's needs may conflict with another's, and both customers' needs may conflict with something you desire internally for your own team. If you are a self-serve business that wants to sell a lightweight product to the masses, you might empathize with companies asking for customizable and configurable features, while realizing that your primary customers want something that works out of the box.

Being in business is being in a state of constantly making trade-offs. Using tools we've talked about previously — such as your shared decision log, proactive knowledge sharing, and optimized OODA Loops — for making informed decisions on these tradeoffs, you will have the basis for a team that will excel in this area. Below are more tips and strategies tailored specifically to this challenge.

Seek feedback — even if it's messy

Imagine working on a product for two years before ever showing it to a customer. Sounds crazy, right? That would be a huge risk. After all that time, you might end up with something that nobody actually wants to use or buy. It's easy to agree on the absurdity of this situation, yet it happens more often than you think.

What causes this tendency for companies to shut themselves off from their customer's point of view?

- Customer feedback has the potential to throw a wrench in your gears. Customers may have contradicting points of view — both with each other, and with you.
- There's a lot of information to sift through. It doesn't always fit into nice, easy categories. And if you bet big on something, there can be a conscious or subconscious desire to see that your plans are not put in jeopardy.
- The perceived potential for many losses — power, autonomy, comfort, security — provokes resistance. Despite outwardly valuing customer feedback, there is often behavioral inertia against it. It's much easier to say, "I'm all for listening to the customer," than it is to actually listen, absorb, and sometimes be wrong.

To build a 10X Culture, you have to be open to feedback from your customers, just like you want to be open to feedback from your team. If your company feels comfortable and no one is challenging its decisions or providing feedback, it has become too insular — and it likely won't grow. Here are a few ways to get more customer feedback to grow your business.

Encourage replies to automated emails. Nearly every email in our new user sequence ends the same way. One or two sentences, in bold type, use some variation of this statement: "We'd love to hear from you. Reply to this email and let us know."

Because our emails are generally written in a casual tone and formatted as if an actual person is sending them, we get a ton of responses on all kinds of topics. We found out one user had made custom tutorial videos so that all of his clients would use Hugo exactly as he wanted. Such dedication! Other times we've found out people are trying to introduce Hugo to others at their company — a great time to step in and provide some resources. So as your first step, go into your email sequences and look for ways to encourage customers to actually respond.

Conduct regular customer interviews. Before making any big decision — such as in our pricing, product roadmap, or content marketing planning — we usually do a round of customer interviews. We'll reach out to five to ten customers and see if they would be willing to chat about their experience with Hugo for thirty minutes in exchange for a modest gift card for their time.

We use a meeting agenda template that includes a lot of general, open-ended questions, which allows the customer to drive the conversation to topics they are most passionate about. The template also delves deep into the heart of why someone is using Hugo and what value they are getting. By launching a series of them before every major decision, we maintain a steady flow of information that helps ensure we have the right perspective.

In the appendix of this book we share this template so you can see exactly how we go about this.

The customer value equation

In its simplest form, **customer value** can be defined as:

$$Value = Benefits - Costs$$

It's not that simple of an equation, though. Both benefits and costs incorporate tangible (quantitative) attributes and intangible (qualitative) ones. Customers assess these categories using both rational and emotional criteria. Despite the equation being so subjective, great companies still work to maximize customer value as best they can. Below are four tips that have worked well for Hugo in untying this Gordian knot.

Plan to make choices. Time and time again, you will have to choose between multiple good ideas. So plan for it. You won't be able to please everyone all the time. Instead of fighting against this, acknowledge it. Understand that tradeoffs are part of the process and that it is better for everyone if you are realistic with your product services or roadmap. Otherwise, you may find yourself overextended, with nobody satisfied.

Follow a specific set of principles. Your company has a mission statement. Your product has a customer value proposition. Your software has a design language. Together, these provide a constellation you can use to guide your decisions.

For example, Hugo's mission is to *connect the way we meet — with the way we work*. Returning to this statement has helped numerous times in making crucial decisions about our product roadmap. When filtered through your company's principles, even challenging decisions often become obvious.

Ask customers to make tradeoffs. Another useful exercise is to involve customers by giving them difficult hypothetical questions. If your product is software, for example, your first instinct might be to softball this. You might ask them to rate a handful of features between one and five. While some ratings may be higher, usually this survey yields a relatively flat curve with few obvious insights.

Instead, up the ante! Ask customers to make tradeoffs. If you could only have one of these two things that you want, which one would it be? Now, instead of a few threes, fours, and fives, your customer has to give you a clear preference.

Calibrate the right amount of focus. When making decisions that will impact your customer base, there are two ditches you can fall into.

The first is focusing too deeply on a single type of customer. Just about every product or service has multiple customer types. This may be varying industries or use cases, or it may be different personas within a company. It's probably a little bit of both. If more than one type of customer is critical for your success, broaden your thinking.

The other common error is doing a little bit of everything — trying to please everyone but in the end pleasing no one. For smaller companies, it is often better to go, as I like to say, five inches wide and five miles deep.

Focus and clarity are a good thing. Just form a hypothesis around where your growth is going to come from, and put your effort into those areas.

16

CAN TECH-TOUCH BE
HIGH-TOUCH?

IN THE PREVIOUS SECTION, we looked at the culture surrounding making decisions for your customers. These are some of the toughest decisions you will have to make.

It can be difficult to decide when and where to provide a personal touchpoint like 1:1 support, and when to automate or use technology to help a larger group of customers at scale. In this section, we'll show you how to combine these strategies for more effective customer relationships overall.

As founders of a SaaS company with customer success embedded in our DNA, we've taken a different approach to CS than most — and it has thus far yielded amazing results.

When you look at how the subscription software economy has exploded, the growth of customer success is no surprise. Customer success managers (CSMs) have become a critical cog in the machine to retain customers, grow accounts, and ensure that customers are consistently receiving value.

But most customer success teams can't grow as fast as their businesses require. To make matters worse, their role is stretched across numerous accounts, and there is a real need to triage customers and allocate time effectively.

This was the origin of the widely accepted approach of categorizing customers as "high-touch," "low-touch," or "no-touch." These labels delineate the degrees of contact, time, and investment spent with particular customers.

- **High-touch** typically means a lot of human time and contact between a dedicated CSM and their clients. This takes the form of personalized emails, phone calls, and meetings.
- **Low-touch** (or mid-touch) means customers are connected to whichever member of the team is available at the moment, or a dedicated CSM sends the occasional check-in email, with limited time spent on the account. CSMs still interact with customers, but typically do not have ownership of particular ones. Where they do, there is limited proactive communication and work done after those communications.
- **No-touch**, as the name suggests, indicates no human contact. No-touch methods include online forms, automated emails, chatbots, and anything else that doesn't require a person working in real-time to support a customer. Many equate "tech-touch" with this category, for obvious — but misguided — reasons. We'll get to that in a moment.

There's a line of thinking that has evolved in customer success that a specific level of touch correlates with a specific customer segment.

Enterprise customers often have the most complex needs, and want solutions fast when a problem arises. They also tend to be proactive, trying to get ahead of problems to prevent them from happening. Most importantly, they have the highest value and revenue potential per customer. Because of this, they are often assigned a CSM dedicated to communicating with and assisting them as needed — which is high-touch.

Mid-market customers need assistance as well, of course, but may not have the same resources or budget as enterprise customers to unlock person-to-person attention. To meet their needs, low- or mid-touch CSM approaches are usually recommended.

Small and medium businesses (SMBs) aren't necessarily producing enough revenue to justify hiring multiple CSMs for them. Because of this, much of customer success management can end up relying on tech touchpoints, or simply having no touchpoints at all, where only automated assistance is provided.

There are a few serious problems with this idea, though:

- Mid-market and SMB customers also want proactive assistance.
- Enterprises and SMBs may enjoy a community forum with answers to common questions and don't always want to talk to someone for a solution or advice.
- Enterprise and mid-market customers can benefit greatly from tech-touch communication, which isn't necessarily low- or no-touch at all.

Wait, are we saying that we send enterprise clients automated emails, or let chatbots handle conversations with them? Yes! We do. It's not as bold as it sounds, because here's the thing: it works.

A customer success manager's task list

From the perspective of a CSM, using tech-touch across the board makes sense. There are only so many working hours in a day to write emails, make phone calls, and attend meetings. If businesses truly value their high-priority customers, one obvious way to improve their experience is to ensure that personalized support is available (or at least appears to be) whenever needed.

A CSM bogged down by emails, calls, and meetings is rarely able to truly communicate with their clients in real-time; they're just too busy. Even when this isn't the case, a customer may reach out to a CSM outside of working hours and have to wait for a reply. In either scenario are customers getting the best quality support?

Tech-touch can do better — especially if some of the questions being answered and problems getting solved are repetitive, meaning initial responses can be instant. Tech-touch should be for repetitive, low-value customer success tasks, freeing up CSMs.

That way, they can do specialized, strategic work, including consulting, giving personalized advice and support, and building meaningful relationships with customers. Imagine how much more freedom they would have to perform these functions if manually addressing basic support issues and follow-ups were taken off their plate.

In short, removing busywork and replacing it with tech-touch enables better customer relationships. Hugo has four additional reasons for using tech-touch across all customer segments:

- **Resourcing**. It's impossible to have "enough" CSMs for a large customer base. The more resources we have, the better.
- **Global customer base**. Because we have customers in multiple time zones, and because our human CSMs are best at being human when they get to sleep on occasion, tech-touch helps us support customers 24/7 until we have full global coverage.
- **Growth rate**. Being experts in tech-touch allows our business to scale much more smoothly. Spikes in sign-ups or a massive expansion in accounts are not as big of an issue.
- **Differentiation**. Doing tech-touch thoughtfully sets us

apart from our competition. We are able to provide better service than others who don't use tech-touch.

Successful tech-touch strategies for all customer segments

Here are our most successful nonstandard, tech-driven strategies that set us apart and, honestly, make our lives easier.

Automated high-touch outreach. One example of our automated communication is an email that gets triggered when a customer is using the Hugo app on the weekend. Using casual language, the email tells the customer that their CSM knows what it's like to have to "catch up" on work over the weekend. It also offers tools that can help streamline that work so that it gets done quicker, leaving more weekend time free.

Of course, our team is hopefully out enjoying their own weekend. But with a little imagination, we have a very personable, high-touch level of service for everyone, not just our enterprise customers during working hours.

Best of all, people reply to these emails (a lot!). We end up having the option to have a lot of engaging exchanges with customers on the weekend — something we don't pass up. But the core of the program is all automatic, which means we just handle the fun part.

As long as it feels like human interaction, these initial tech-touches can be just as good as the real thing for many customers. And best of all, customer success now has an inbox full of customers to respond to, rather than the far more difficult, time-consuming task of outreach to start conversations.

Proactive support. The idea that proactivity should be limited to high-level customers just isn't true. Businesses of all sizes want to get ahead of issues, and we use automated, personalized messages to communicate how we help them do that.

When our error logging software detects that a customer has just experienced a bug while using Hugo, for example, they receive a friendly message from us. This message communicates that we noticed an error occurred and that we are looking into it — and our system is, in fact, doing that — without human assistance.

This is arguably even more proactive than a human CSM, who might not be aware that a customer experienced an error until the customer communicates it. Even if an automated alert is sent to the CSM, it may not get addressed until it's a distant memory for the customer.

THE "WELCOME TO HUGO" swag pack. Perhaps the most fun tech-touch we do is one that uses tech to provide some real-world goodies for customers to enjoy: swag!

After signing up and achieving in-product goals, new Hugo customers are sent a package with Hugo t-shirts, socks, and helpful content for their team to learn new methods of teamwork and business growth. You may have received this book as part of one of these bundles.

This very high-touch service is completely automated — so all customers get a red carpet experience. There is no human time cost, and our customers are each reminded that we value them.

The new frontier of tech-touch

Tech-touch is no longer about "low" or "high" touch; it's about employing tools, processes, and technology to be more proactive and available, and removing busywork for CSMs. This maximizes their time spent in high-value relationship building and consulting — true value-adds for customers.

Customer success management is the hub to the many spokes in a business. Without happy customers, a business can't scale; and without capturing and centralizing customer insights, the rest of the business can't be truly customer-centric.

Scaling customer success is a pain point many of our clients approach us with. With our Connected Meeting Notes software powering CSM teams globally, our goal at Hugo is to maximize value from customer conversations — which counterintuitively means using automation to start a lot of those communications.

SUMMARY: 10X CUSTOMERS

- Your customers are an intrinsic part of your team culture. How you approach customer relationships is an important factor in your success.
- Encourage knowledge-sharing about your customers in your organization, ensuring that even people who don't work with customers daily have a clear understanding of who your customers are and what they need.
- Plan to make difficult tradeoffs on behalf of your customers. Use principles such as your value proposition to make these decisions easier.
- Use tech-driven touchpoints to increase the frequency and personalization of your customer success efforts, especially in ways where tech-touch leads to personal touch when it matters.

V

---

10 X MEETINGS

Want to get a quick read on your company culture? Just look at your *meetings*. It's all there: the interpersonal relationships, the power dynamics, the team camaraderie. For many organizations, meetings are a reflection of the company's broader processes and health.

At Hugo, we have seen this firsthand. The company was founded on the idea that we could make meetings more effective. The more we worked to change our meetings for the better, the more we noticed a correlating positive effect in other aspects of how we worked.

It makes sense, right? Meetings are where decisions get made. They are where knowledge gets shared. Nearly everything important that happens in a company originates from something that happens in a meeting.

Whether the meetings are in-person, remote, or somewhere in between, the way we meet has a profound effect on the way we work. That's why, in order to build a stronger team culture, you're going to have to tackle one of the most sensitive, controversial processes in your organization: *meetings*.

Meetings can be a colossal waste of time. And if people leave meetings feeling drained and demoralized — as if their time was wasted — then meetings might also be your biggest expense. But that doesn't have to be the case.

Meetings can be a place where you set the stage for your 10X Culture — a public, team-driven confirmation of the good habits that you are trying to build. Whether you lead meetings or just participate, your role there echoes into the rest of the company.

To start our journey into 10X Meetings, let's first look at an innovation Steve Jobs created — not an iPod with touch controls, not a revolutionary mobile phone, not even a breakthrough internet communications device. This Steve Jobs invention relates purely to meetings.

17

THE ONE THING STEVE JOBS SAYS EVERY MEETING NEEDS

PEOPLE VOICE three main complaints about meetings:

- *We have too many.*
- *They are a waste of time.*
- *Nothing ever gets done.*

Steve Jobs figured out a way to eliminate two out of the three.

If you feel that you're having the same conversations over and over again, or that nothing gets done as a result of meetings, you and your team may not be reaching closure on each topic. Closure comes from determining and communicating the next steps. It can be achieved by sending out a summary of the meeting within an hour of attending — or at least before the end of the day.

But the key element to closure, which Jobs keenly uncovered, is responsibility. In Walter Isaacson's biography of Steve Jobs, he tells the story of Apple's struggle to foster a culture of accountability within teams. Many people felt their success or failure was caused by external forces, and especially by other people.

Jobs wanted to instill a sense of personal responsibility; he didn't want to hear excuses, especially from other leaders in his organization. So when it came to meetings, he set up a policy that made sure there wouldn't be any excuses available. His solution was the Directly Responsible Individual (DRI).

Isaacson writes:

> "Steve had a habit of making sure someone was responsible for each item on any meeting agenda, so everybody knew who is responsible . . . An effective meeting at Apple will have an action list . . . Next to each action item will be the DRI."

When we combine the idea of a DRI with the need for closure on discussion topics, we find the solution to two of the three biggest problems with meetings. When meetings are a waste of time, it is *because* nothing gets done. Setting clear action items, then explicitly confirming that a single person is responsible, is the solution.

Why assigning DRIs works so well

At first, declaring that someone is directly responsible for every task or project may feel like it adds too much bureaucracy or micromanagement to your workflow. Is it really necessary? Can't people just work the way they want to work?

The truth is that this tiny upfront investment yields disproportionate returns. In fact, appointing a DRI removes many other time-consuming activities from work. That allows employees to do their best work on what they should be working on — and nothing else. Rather than sapping productivity, assigning a DRI *enables* it. Here are four reasons why:

- **DRIs encourage autonomy.** When you're the responsible individual, you are not dependent on a manager to tell you what to do. This makes teams and leaders more self-reliant. It also allows people to automatically organize around the DRI without having to first traffic-cop their way through company bureaucracy.

- **DRIs permit teamwork.** When it's unclear what should be happening, everyone can trust that the DRI is in the driver's seat. If the DRI is quiet, what needs to get done must be getting done.
- **DRIs enable efficiency.** Because each issue has only a single person worrying about it, the mental resources of your organization can be spread much more widely.
- **DRIs require specificity.** While assigning someone to be responsible, you must be clear about what they are *responsible for*. Specificity on projects, tasks, and action items brings necessary focus to team activities.

When to establish a DRI

To speed up decision-making and heighten accountability, assign the DRI early. Here are two important times to do so:

1. When working on a new or complex problem where the owner is not yet known.
2. At the end of meetings, when leaving with action items or next steps.

Even if the DRI is implied, verbally confirm it out loud. For example, "Rob will put together the product launch plan this week, and I'll follow up with our PR agency." If you're in a meeting, write the DRI's name next to every action item in your notes. Better still, if your actions are sent to project management software, assign the action to the DRI in that software (at Hugo, we use Asana and Trello for this).

Now, having tackled two of the main complaints about meetings, it's time to move on to the last: too many meetings that are too long.

18

THE 4-HOUR MEETING WEEK

MY FIRST DAY at Hugo was a breeze. Then Josh told me about the " 1 o Percent Rule."

"This week you're ramping up, so we have a lot of meetings," he said, in his Australian accent that to me sounds just like Chris Hemsworth. "After this, though, block off no more than four hours per forty-hour week for internal meetings. This is how we move fast."

If your CEO told you — in Thor's voice, no less — to keep your meetings under four hours a week, what would you do? You might be peeking at your calendar right now, saying, "But I have four hours of meetings . . . *today!*"

At first, I thought it was an impossible goal too. Plenty of people have closer to four hours of *non*-meetings each week during working hours. With that perspective, the 1 o-Hour Rule at Hugo might be perplexing. We make Connected Meeting Notes software. Shouldn't the company that invests in making meetings more effective be having even more meetings than average?

Now let's be clear — we love meetings. But do you know what we love more than meetings? Progress. Getting stuff done. We love how fast an organization can move when every day isn't carved into check-ins and sync-ups and stand-ups and sit-downs.

So how do you figure out how to have only the most effective meetings possible? To start, you reduce or eliminate the majority of your meetings. Here are five ways your organization can cut down on meetings while keeping the ones that move the company forward.

Share updates in advance

One of the most common words in any meeting agenda is "update." More than one in five agendas created with our software contain it. An update is just a concise explanation of where something is at and what has changed. Three minutes of updates can easily fit into three written bullet points.

But live updates in meetings take so much longer than that, and there's a social reason for it: If you can explain your progress in twenty seconds, your work looks unimportant. Whether intentional or not, people include unnecessary levels of detail in updates.

If your entire meeting is updates, have everyone share three bullet points and read each other's notes. Only have a meeting if that surfaces anything to discuss. Otherwise, skip the meeting!

If there are discussions to be had, you already have updates out of the way. Everyone should show up to the meeting prepared. Your long, thirty-minute discussion trims down to a quick, efficient ten, without wasting time on getting everyone on the same page.

Make a video instead

Sometimes having a meeting seems as if it would be more efficient. It takes less time to explain something in person than to write it all down. But when you make a habit of this, the default method for sharing information becomes . . . yet another meeting.

If you think the discussion will be less than fifteen minutes, just make a quick video instead. When you make a video, you get your point across without risking misinterpretation. And because it's asynchronous communication, the people on the other end can respond when they're available and on their own schedule — even if they're in another time zone.

Loom is a free tool to record and privately share videos that can include both your webcam and your screen. While Loom comes in handy, videos can seem too permanent. Once you start recording, you begin to invest time in making the best video possible.

To combat this, we created an internal tool called Fade — the child of Loom and Snapchat. Fade videos are simple to make, but they self-destruct after seven days. There's no more worrying if you make a minor mistake. As in real life, the experience is there — and then it's gone.

Just don't go to the meeting

If you're in a cross-functional or managerial role, you may feel obligated to go to a lot of meetings. You need to stay up to date on everything. It's not that you're a necessary presenter; you're just worried that you might miss an important detail. But when you sit through meetings that are irrelevant to you, you waste your own time.

What you need is excellent, high-level meeting notes consistently delivered to you. Ideally, these notes are in a centralized place — not some coworker's scratchpad or random folder. We post our meeting notes to Slack. Skip the meeting, and ask for notes instead.

Stand up for stand-ups

It's popular to describe ultra-brief meetings as stand-ups. We've noticed, though, that if anyone is remote, stand-ups quickly become sit-downs, if they weren't already. The point of calling it a stand-up is that you get tired if it goes on too long. So stay standing.

Adopt ad hoc meetings

The real secret in sticking to our 10 Percent Rule at Hugo is that we still work together all the time. We just have very few formal meetings.

For example, a manager might ask someone if they can chat about a design. They get on a videoconference, have a conversation, and get it taken care of in eight minutes instead. By not blocking off an arbitrary thirty minutes, the discussion gets done in exactly the time required.

You can debate whether that example technically constitutes a meeting. Yes, it used videoconference software. Yes, it had a mutually agreed–upon time (right now!). But we don't count these against our 10 Percent Rule. By encouraging everyone to work together in a more ad hoc manner, meeting times are compressed to the minimum time required.

Whether or not it is feasible to get all the way down to the 10 Percent Rule at your company isn't the real issue here. Every company is different — and keep in mind that this is for internal meetings only. We don't count time spent with customers against the quota because, as we've talked about, those conversations are crucial for leveling up our customer understanding.

The combination of the 10 Percent Rule with how we use Slack and Fade increases our awareness about how we spend our time. It reflects a commitment to not wasting people's time when other communication options are more effective and efficient. By reclaiming some of that time, we can put it into the work that drives results. And because we combine the 10 Percent Rule with always assigning DRIs, we never have too many meetings, they're never a waste of time, and something always gets done.

We've solved for the three main meeting complaints. But we didn't stop there, because we didn't just want meetings to be *not bad*. We wanted them to be *great*. To be moments when our collective skills and energies would come together. To be the very forum that would propel our business forward. And we were successful. We did it by using a simple methodology for making decisions — which you will learn in the next chapter.

19

WHEN THE BEST IDEAS WIN

At Hugo, we consider meetings to be a common operating system for teamwork. If we can innovate around how we collaborate, we can turn meetings into a new way of working that gives us a competitive advantage.

One advantage we have developed comes from the way that we share information and make decisions in meetings. It's a process that helps ensure that meetings always surface our best ideas. To illustrate this, let's look at a troublesome, unsolved problem that threatened to cancel the first trip to the moon.

The Saturn V rocket that delivered the Apollo mission to the moon was — and still is — the tallest, heaviest, most powerful (by total impulse) rocket ever brought to operational status. At 310,000 lbs (140,000 kgs), its record-breaking heaviest, largest payload included the Apollo command and service module and lunar modules — and the propellant needed to send them to the moon.

While this spacefaring giant was being manufactured in a Vehicle Assembly Building not far from the launch pad, the Apollo team faced a challenge of similar proportions to the rocket itself: how to transport it there.

A vehicle that massive had never been made. The rocket stood as high as a thirty-six-story building — 363 feet tall (111 m). Even without fins, it was thirty-three feet in diameter (10 m), or about five times as wide as a normal car. Without fuel, the Saturn V weighed a mere 525,500 pounds (239,725 kg). There were no store-bought solutions to this problem.

To keep up with their accelerated timeline, NASA began construction of the rocket before they had a strategy to move it. All of the work that thousands of people were doing to send a man to the moon would be wasted if they couldn't even get the rocket to the launch pad.

Solutions often come from curious places. In the case of Saturn V, despite world-class engineering teams agonizing over how to overcome the challenge, the winning idea didn't come from an engineer at all.

The solution was an enormous "crawler-transporter." Part aircraft carrier, part tank, and weighing in at a svelte six million pounds (2.7 million kg), the crawler-transporter holds its own world record: as the largest self-propelled land vehicle.

The marvelous idea for the crawler-transporter, which was used for more than thirty years, came from a member of the launch operations team, whose name is now lost to history. They got the idea for it after watching the strip-mining process. The solution for landing man on the moon came from the science of traveling in the opposite direction — excavating deep inside the planet.

Every challenge in business has the potential for *to-the-moon* levels of complexity. The ingenuity and creativity to solve these problems can come from anywhere, but only if you encourage ideas from all elements of the workforce. That means being transparent about challenges, and actively listening to people — even if they are discussing topics outside of their area of specialty.

This practice — acting as an *idea meritocracy* — is a secret weapon that can help you make better decisions and solve hard problems more quickly. Simply put, an idea meritocracy is an environment in which the best idea wins. We didn't come up with this idea on our own; companies such as Pixar, Intuit, and Google have adopted idea meritocracies with great success.

In their book *How Google Works*, Eric Schmidt, former CEO of Google, and Jonathan Rosenberg, former Google senior vice president of products, discussed why they embrace the power of an idea meritocracy: "In most companies, experience is the winning argument. We call these places 'tenurocracies,' because power derives from tenure, not merit . . . Meritocracies yield better decisions and create an environment where all employees feel valued and empowered."

In his book *Principles*, Ray Dalio outlines how to turn your organization into an idea meritocracy. Dalio says **meaningful work** and **meaningful relationships** are cultural precursors to operating as an idea meritocracy. Dalio also suggests you operate with **radical straightforwardness**, a combination of truthfulness and transparency where you deal with issues openly. In our organization, we call this *absolute honesty*.

In daily practice, we've found there are two other requirements to being an idea meritocracy. One is **thoughtful disagreements**. When you have thoughtful disagreements, it means there are reasonable back-and-forths in which people evolve their thinking to come up with better decisions than they could have come up with individually.

It's also helpful to have **disagreement protocols** to help people get past disagreements in idea-meritocratic ways. One example of disagreement protocols is to use a weighted vote, where the DRI has 3x the weight, those affected by the decision in terms of area of responsibility have 2x, and all other attendees have 1x. Another is to involve an external arbitrator. This could be someone from another team, who comes in when there is disagreement on what is the best decision, listens to the data, and makes a final decision.

If the concept of an idea meritocracy makes you feel both excited and uncomfortable, you're not alone. Yes, it can be challenging on an emotional level, as it requires vulnerability and humility from everyone involved. But ask yourself what kind of work environment you want to craft for yourself and your team. Then try answering the following questions:

- Do you want your team to make the best decisions?
- Do you want your team to constantly improve and innovate?
- Do you want your employees to be more highly engaged and become the best thinkers and learners that they can be?
- Do you want your organization to be more proactive, agile, and adaptive?

If so, becoming an idea meritocracy might be for you and your team.

Idea meritocracy in action

It sounds almost utopian! But here's the tough part: In an idea meritocracy, how do you decide which idea is best?

First, let's look at how you *don't* decide. In an idea meritocracy, factors such as positional power, pay, and even experience become nearly irrelevant compared to objective measures, such as the quantity and quality of data and how it is interpreted.

To help determine which idea is best, Ray Dalio suggests you start by addressing your own opinion as one of many. Then ask yourself how you know whether or not your opinion is right. This will help shift your perspective by focusing your attention on the right criteria to make this decision. Dalio says this eliminates "one of the greatest tragedies of mankind . . . people arrogantly, naïvely holding opinions in their minds that are wrong, and acting on them, and not putting them out there to stress test them."

Now that you're viewing all ideas on the same level, come to a decision in a "believability-weighted way." Do this by determining an idea's legitimacy based on the track record and the ability of the idea's originator to clearly explain their concept. If and when a disagreement arises, start by agreeing on the principles used to make the decision, and then explore the merits of the reasoning behind each principle.

Plant the seeds of idea meritocracy in your meetings

By now, you might be wondering why a chapter on ideas is in 10X Meetings and not somewhere else, like 10X Decision-Making. The reason is that while updating our worldview of meeting culture to be consistent with the way we work, we found meetings to be the perfect place to establish and reinforce the principles of being an idea meritocracy.

Here are a few other practices and ideas to consider as you implement idea meritocracy in your meetings:

1. Team member contributions should not be defined by what they know or how much they know — but rather by the quality of their thinking, listening, learning, and collaborating.
2. Mental models are not the same as reality — at best, they are generalized ideas about how the world works.
3. Ideas do not equal ego. To have a right idea or a wrong idea is not to *be* right or to *be* wrong.
4. Treat all beliefs as hypotheses to be constantly tested and subject to change based on better data.
5. Mistakes and failures are opportunities to learn.

Conventional business thinking favors factors such as job title and seniority as a measure of idea value. That's why startups that can overlook those factors can beat out established incumbent businesses.

Surfacing the best ideas is as simple as choosing the right principles, processes, and tools.

This new way of working presents an opportunity for fast-moving teams to outperform others by leveraging the ideas of their whole team — including remote workers and decentralized teams.

One of our most valuable strategies at Hugo is to have many brains working on our greatest challenges based on information sharing across the business. Ideas often come from people on our team who aren't directly responsible for the solution.

You might think this philosophy conflicts in some way with our advice about having a DRI for every task or project, but it doesn't. Even if someone owns a bit of work, the team is there to back them up. If you need input or a sounding board, or just want to question your own assumptions, there are other ideas and perspectives at your disposal. That's how combining a culture of knowledge-sharing with an idea meritocracy unlocks so much potential for solutions, feedback, and opportunities from every aspect of the business.

20

THE GLUE THAT HOLDS MEETINGS AND WORK TOGETHER

So FAR, we've explored how to solve the biggest complaints about meetings. We've looked at how to transform decision-making by initiating an idea meritocracy. We've looked at tactical tips, such as the 10 Percent Rule, and Steve Jobs' DRI concept.

It's fitting, then, to end on a topic that connects all of these ideas together — a simple, powerful tool for transforming your meeting culture. The good news is that this is something you probably already do, at least some of the time. But we're going to teach you why and how you can do it better to transform the way you work. It's a toolkit that is simple, practical, and always useful.

We're talking about the words and artifacts that surround your meetings: your meeting agendas, and your meeting notes themselves. Both of these powerfully contribute to your meeting culture, and when used effectively, can reinforce the values of your organization.

How to use agendas to encourage participation

Every meeting should have a purpose, a goal, a reason for each attendee to be there. Your roadmap to achieving that goal is your agenda.

The traditional way to plan a meeting is for the host to put together the entire agenda. Usually, agenda-setting is one person deciding on their own how they want to use thirty or sixty minutes of other people's time.

This strategy lacks collaboration. Other meeting participants aren't given an opportunity to influence the meeting. Any insights or innovations they might bring to its structure are lost. Having a single person fully control the agenda of a meeting stifles participation from the other attendees.

We propose a superior approach: whenever possible, agendas should be a team effort. That means they should be made in a collaborative format, shared with all attendees as the agenda is coming together.

Discussion topics, objectives, and other agenda items may still be dictated by the meeting's host, to some degree. But what if a team member is giving updates? Ask them in advance to summarize them in bullet points in the agenda. If a discussion requires some information to kick it off, have the experts in that area contribute that information to the agenda in advance.

Collaborative agendas are one of the most powerful workflow hacks that we have discovered at Hugo. When you encourage participation before the meeting even starts, people are more likely to show up prepared, enthusiastic, and engaged with the meeting. After all, they helped plan it.

In early 2019, someone who was using Hugo for meeting notes and agendas reached out to us. She told us that sharing agendas had given her a voice in her organization. As a quieter female in a male-dominated tech company, she often felt subdued in meetings, unable to contribute at the same level as people who were louder or more assertive than her. But something as simple as getting on the agenda gave her new influence on the direction the meeting would go — and set her up as a speaker, as well.

All types of people in your organization may not be able to participate equally in discussions and decision-making. There are probably dynamics that you don't even realize. Issues of gender, race, age, seniority, introversion or extroversion, or even a friendly relationship with the person leading the meeting can limit your meeting culture and the discussions that happen in your meeting. Shared meeting agendas provide a way to promote a more equal share of voice.

Putting decisions into action

How you record and follow up on meeting discussions also has cultural implications. Your meeting notes are not just records of what transpired; they're often an implicit contract with what was decided. In fact, if you are using the DRI technique covered earlier, then every action item that comes out of your meeting will already have a directly responsible individual.

But good notetaking does not just include action items. It's a general best practice to also log decisions. For any discussion topic on an agenda, often the only note that counts is the one that says what the outcome was. This acts as a sort of mini decision log for all the smaller decisions you're making in the meeting.

Why is it so important to make note of decisions as they are made?

First, the act of writing decisions down helps you commit to them. Earlier in the book, we suggested that you try to reduce or eliminate usage of the word "should" to help you avoid being noncommittal; writing down decisions provides a similar outcome. It's a way of confirming that a discussion topic has been settled. It's definitive, final, and now clear to everyone at the meeting that it's time to move on.

Writing your decisions in your meeting notes is also a good way to remind yourself about whether or not the rest of the team needs to be alerted to an issue. So many decisions impact so many people and departments, yet it takes days, weeks — months, sometimes — for information to make its way across the company. But when you log a decision in your notes, it's now in a document along with the rest of your notes which can easily be shared with your team, whether that be in chat, email, or on your meeting notes platform. So share those notes!

Increasing transparency by sharing meeting notes is an example of proactive sharing, the kind of radical straightforwardness that gives team members the additional perspective and context they need to make great decisions. When decisions are logged in your notes and shared, suddenly other teams in your company become aware of changes that may affect them and their own thinking.

Finally, shared notes are a great way to hit the 10 Percent Rule. So much meeting attendance has to do with business-related FOMO — just think about what kind of important information might be missed! Remove that fear through good notetaking and sharing, and suddenly everyone will be a lot more comfortable with putting the time and effort that would've gone into that meeting into another activity — an activity that might actually help 10X your business.

21

THE JERK, THE SLACKER, AND THE DOWNER

WORKING TOGETHER IS HARD ENOUGH. What would you do if somebody was actively — and secretly — trying to undermine everything your team did? In his book *The Culture Code,* Daniel Coyle tells about a researcher in Australia who hired an actor to sabotage teamwork.

For his experiment, Will Felps, who studies organizational behavior at the University of New South Wales in Australia, gathered forty groups of four. He gave each group a task. Into each group, he inserted a fifth team member, an actor named Nick, whose responsibility was to mess them up.

Nick's job was to play one of three negative archetypes: the Jerk, the Slacker, and the Downer. The Jerk is aggressive and defiant. The Slacker doesn't put in the effort. And the Downer is a pessimistic type — think Eeyore from Winnie the Pooh.

It turned out that it didn't matter precisely how Nick attempted to disrupt the group. In almost every instance, Nick was able to kill the group's performance, tanking it by at least 30 percent. A single outlier group, though, confounded Nick and Dr. Felps. Here's what Felps said:

> *They first came to my attention when Nick mentioned*
> *that there was one group that felt really different to him .*
> *. . The group performed well, no matter what he did.*
> *Nick said it was mostly because of one guy.*

Before we talk about that one guy, let's talk about the destruction Nick sowed on his teams. Felps' research shows the profound effect even one individual can have on stymieing productivity, innovation, and cooperation. Whether or not they appreciate it, these negative, team-sabotaging behaviors, if left unchecked, can stifle your organization.

It also stands to reason that the opposite may be true. While we don't have an additional study from Felps where Nick plays the Nice Guy, the Hard Worker, or the Glass Half-Full Guy, it follows that having positive people on your team could produce the opposite result. The extraordinary guy referred to in Felps' quote above seemed to have traits of all three of those positive archetypes.

His name is Jonathan. With curly hair and a natural smile, Jonathan is a thin, unimposing young man who speaks with a quiet and steady voice.

Jonathan is up against Nick, the Jerk. However, whenever Nick tries to be overly assertive and aggressive, Jonathan defuses the situation. He does this calmly and repeatedly. Felps studied the video of their interactions over and over again, analyzing them like a forensic scientist. As you may have expected, Felps found that Jonathan followed a pattern.

Whenever Nick started to get negative, Jonathan would react warmly. Felps said:

> *Nick would start being a jerk, and [Jonathan] would lean*
> *forward, use body language, laugh and smile — never in*
> *a contemptuous way, but in a way that takes the danger*
> *out of the room and defuses the situation. It doesn't seem*

all that different at first. When you look more closely, it
causes some incredible things to happen.

What Jonathan was doing was transforming an unstable dynamic into a reliable, safe environment. He would deflect negative energy and turn the conversation back toward positivity. He would ask simple questions to help others open up and share ideas, and then listen intently and respond to them. People's energy would increase.

What can we learn from this unimposing peacemaker? Participants' behaviors can profoundly impact meetings and teamwork in general. Even if someone is having an off day, it's not a done deal. When negativity starts to seep in, it just takes another person — a force for good — to act as a counterbalance. Simple changes in behavior can have significant consequences, and over the next few chapters, we'll examine how to harness that potential.

When some of the most critical decisions in business are being made collaboratively in these environments, we must all be our best. In the case of Felps' experiment, the participants were performing a simple, measurable task. In real meetings, it's often more complicated than that.

The objective may be to set the strategy for an upcoming quarter. It could be to decide what to do about a new competitor. It could be deciding the approach for a new challenge or how much to invest in helping your neediest customer. The objectives here are not so clear-cut and easily measured, but the outcome of every one of them is critical to your overall success. If it wasn't, why would you be having a meeting about it in the first place?

So keep an eye out for these negative archetypes in your meetings. If you encounter one, here are a few more strategies for counteracting their negative influence.

Don't engage with negativity

Toxic negativity is infectious. It's very easy to go negative yourself in an attempt to counterbalance it. Instead, maintain your emotional distance. A difficult individual is locked into a negative mindset. They are likely to put pressure and demands on those around them. Don't engage on those terms.

When you do interact with their negativity, do so with noncommittal language. You want to acknowledge what someone is saying without endorsing their ideas. Agree with what you can. Then, rephrase their complaints using less loaded and more realistic language — as Jonathan would.

Hold your tongue

Jerks and downers often behave that way because they're looking for a reaction. Responding in anger or frustration only feeds their negativity. But to get through the situation, you're still going to have to do *something*.

Try to listen without being judgmental. Buried deep underneath their behavior is likely a valid point, so look for it. When you find what they are trying to say, respond, but keep it objective and emotional. Explain your response with care and thought.

Take charge of the conversation

One of the skills that our hero Jonathan practiced is refocusing and reframing conversations, even as Nick tried to disrupt. You can defuse a conversation and guide it toward more neutral or positive topics by gently acknowledging what someone is saying and then moving on to a new or different take on the subject, or a new subject entirely.

Here are a few reframing examples:

- **Shift from negative to positive.** For negative comments, you might offer an alternate point of view. "I'm also frustrated the campaign didn't produce the leads we were hoping for. On the bright side, we got off easy. We learned a valuable lesson for just a few hundred dollars in advertising."
- **Shift from passive to active.** If someone says, "We've always been behind that competitor. I don't see how we can catch up," you might respond, "What are some activities we can do today to close that gap?"
- **Shift from assumptions to facts.** If a discussion dives too deep into negative ideas that are hypothetical, you might say, "It sounds like we may have churned those customers because of what you just mentioned. But many factors influence churn, including many that are out of our control. Is this something we want to look into more, or just keep an eye on for the time being?"

Be enthusiastic

The best defense against negativity is often positivity. It's exhausting to relentlessly act out around people who are passionate, positive, and genuine. Small, friendly gestures can chip away at someone's doom and gloom. Their outlook may not transform overnight, but just as their negativity wears others down, your positivity might brighten them up.

Don't let this cautionary tale about the worst of the worst — the Jerks, Slackers, and Downers — distract you from the upside of great meetings: Meetings that take up the right amount of time in your week. Meetings where everyone has a voice, where the best ideas win, and where the process that you use to conduct the meeting itself leads to more engaged participation and better results.

SUMMARY: 10X MEETINGS

- Using Steve Jobs' technique, assign every project and action item to a directly responsible individual (DRI).
- Give your team more time to do their work by removing unnecessary meetings. Record a short video in place of a basic meeting. Collaborate on agendas in advance to shorten meetings.
- Encourage your team to be an idea meritocracy during meeting discussions. Make space for contributions, even from unlikely sources.
- Take a collaborative approach to meeting agendas to encourage buy-in from all attendees and to provide an equitable voice to participants.
- Encourage transparency. Share meeting notes publicly when possible, listing discussions, decisions, and action items.
- Negative influences like the Jerk, the Slacker, and the Downer can decimate meeting productivity. A positive meeting environment, on the other hand, is part of a 10X Culture.

VI

10 X REMOTE

The shift toward distributed teams and remote workers is one of the most underreported workplace transformations in recent years. According to a 2018 Upwork study, 63 percent of U.S. companies now have remote workers among their employees.

The rising prevalence of remote work poses unique challenges for team culture. In many ways, remote work is far less intimate. There are fewer opportunities to socialize — an essential activity that builds culture and rapport among team members.

As a remote worker, you have to be intentional about every interaction you want to have with colleagues. You can't walk by a conversation and jump in, as you might in a traditional workplace. And if you work with remote team members, the same goes for you; it's easy to forget about your out-of-sight colleagues.

According to an FYI Remote Work report, the top three challenges facing remote workers are:

1. Communication (27 percent)
2. Social opportunities (16 percent)
3. Loneliness and isolation (13 percent)

If you work in the same building as your entire team, you might think that a discussion on remote work does not apply to you. With the way that organizations operate today, though, even people working fifty feet apart often experience the same challenges as remote workers. Coworkers send each other messages on chat or email. They collaborate on virtual documents. Yes, you have the option of walking over to someone's desk and saying hello. *But do you?*

All of the challenges remote workers and their onsite colleagues encounter can be overcome, or at least managed, with 10X Culture. In this section, we will examine ways that we've learned to help each other thrive, even when we are distributed. These tips apply whether teams are fifty feet apart, on the next floor, or in a different time zone altogether.

22

A NEW LENS FOR REMOTE WORK

MELANIE WORKED as part of my marketing team while I was based in San Francisco. When I moved to Seattle, she stayed on as my direct report. Suddenly, I was faced with effectively managing someone who no longer sat five feet from me.

But a few weeks in, during one of our routine calls, it struck me that our working relationship had become more effective because of the distance. At first I thought this was counterintuitive, but it wasn't. The distance forced us to be smarter about their interactions. We were more stringent with planning ahead of time. We communicated better overall because I couldn't rely on just waving my hand to get Melanie's attention.

Since then, I've worked remotely in some capacity, including being a full-time remote employee at Hugo. In that time, I've done a lot of reading and soul-searching about how to build a healthy distributed work culture. This section contains what I've found to be the keys to successfully working remotely. It doesn't just apply to full-time employees — relationships with freelancers, contractors, agencies, and advisers can also benefit from this advice.

Multimodal communication

Recall our earlier discussion about high- versus low-bandwidth communication. Face-to-face communication is the highest possible bandwidth. Asynchronous text (e.g., email) is the lowest.

When working remotely, it's easy to default to low-bandwidth modes of communication. It can feel intrusive to ask for face time with someone who works 2,000 miles away. But the most effective remote teams develop good habits around multimodal communication, optimizing their communication modes for the right bandwidth and type of discussion needed.

Embracing a multimodal approach allows you to balance the overall bandwidth of information transfer with people's preferences, calibrating your organization to excel. Full-spectrum communication is critical to having a capable remote team.

Another benefit of using the most appropriate type of communication is that it helps you have the right amount of interaction. Remote teams need to be aligned to be productive, but too many interruptions break productivity. A fifteen-minute phone call can save you an hour of back and forth on Slack.

A new model of accountability

In the old way of doing business, job performance was measured by how much time you spent behind a desk. If you were the first to arrive and last to leave, you were a superstar.

Remote work flips that entire notion on its head. Teams measure performance by results and impact, not time in the seat. Successful remote teams embrace this disruption, rather than fight against it.

This paradigm shift comes into play massively with freelancers, whose rates are often project-based, not hourly. The cover art for this book was commissioned at a flat rate. It was then up to Zoe to complete the project, on her terms, knowing the outcome we wanted from her. Whether she painted it on a tablet in Starbucks or in her home studio at 3 a.m. while re-watching the entire Harry Potter series was totally up to her. We measured success by the completion of an illustration that was unique, bold, and evocative — and Zoe knocked it out of the park.

These changes don't just affect freelancers, though. Full-time remote workers operate on a similar, if more complicated basis. All remote workers have much greater ownership over how they are going to approach their tasks. For many, that is what enables them to be so successful.

So rather than measuring time-at-desk with a stopwatch, set clear guidelines and expectations. At Hugo, we use task management software and collaborative documents to organize our plans. Action items, due dates, and work are easy to access and update, no matter where you are located.

Approaching work in this way gives you the freedom to allow more flexibility. For example, one engineer on our team uses a polyphasic sleep cycle. While he sleeps fewer hours than most people overall, he's sometimes not awake in the middle of the day — and sometimes he's hard at work in the middle of the night.

By remaining flexible with the arrangements that can help remote workers thrive, you can provide an even higher value in the remote opportunity. Every worker is unique — and that uniqueness can be either stifled, to the company's detriment, or it can be leveraged, to the company's benefit. It's a win-win.

Embrace casual communication

Widespread adoption of new communication modes over the last few decades has changed both the mode and the form in which we communicate using the Internet. The neutral, objective, stuffy patterns of professional communication from the past have gradually given way to a more intimate, human, and casual tone for most businesses.

These new patterns of communication have not just been a shift in tone. Emojis, once considered casual and just for teenagers, are now part of mainstream culture. They provide a necessary additional layer of information in text-based communication, where we don't have body language and facial expressions as cues.

GIFs and memes abound, providing people at work with ways to describe feelings and ideas that are instant and visual. Acronyms like "smh" (shaking my head) and the ubiquitous "lol" (laughing out loud) provide a quick shorthand to these otherwise-physical interactions.

For some, adopting these trends might not come easily; it may be a struggle to embrace them. But when you do, it will allow you to communicate more effectively with people every day. And because we're often interacting remotely, all these fist bumps ( ) and thank you's ( ) are essential. They stand in for in-person high fives or the smile and nod you give when saying "thank you," when you genuinely mean it.

When receiving emojis and GIFs, remain open-minded. Remote communication, even when done well, can still be plagued with misunderstandings. You often don't have the full context. In an office, you might be able to figure out that Darren barely got any sleep because of his new baby pretty quickly. However, if you're trading emails and Slack messages with him, the puffy eyes and fourth cup of coffee aren't going to be as noticeable.

Always assume good intentions. For example, there are multiple ways to interpret an emoji. It can indicate sarcasm. It can also suggest silliness. If you find yourself interpreting communication negatively, stop and consider whether you are reading the situation correctly, and with a mind that is open to good intentions.

Remote workers want career growth too

Often unintentionally, remote workers are not given access to the same career opportunities that their office-based coworkers are. Being out of sight can make it hard for a remote worker to level up. Even people who consistently put out good work can be overlooked in favor of people who are seen showing up to the office every day.

So it's crucial to offer continued training, development, and growth opportunities for remote workers. Even if no promotion is likely to occur, people must not feel stagnant in their position. If you supervise remote teammates, schedule time periodically to think about their career growth, or make it a recurring agenda item for your regular one-on-ones.

Treat everyone as remote

There's an easy way to ensure you don't end up with an "us versus them" culture of in-office versus remote workers: treat everyone as remote, regardless of their location. That means that if a remote worker is on-camera in a meeting, ideally everyone else is too, whether that be on one large group cam, or a few individual ones — provided your Internet bandwidth can handle such excess.

Treating all work as remote work is a helpful way to lead by example. Don't expect remote workers to embody the best practices of communication if no one in the proper office is doing it. When you share freely and communicate often, regardless of your location, that will become the norm for your team. And who knows — just like I experienced with Melanie, these practices might improve your overall communication.

23

WHEN GOOD ENOUGH IS NOT ENOUGH

There's one more aspect of working with remote team members that should be non-negotiable. If you can't do it, everything else will be slower, more complicated, and less productive. It's an area where complacency or settling for something that seems to be "good enough" can present a real danger.

Ask yourself a simple question: Does everyone on your team have the tools they need to get their job done? Your immediate answer is likely, *Yes, of course they do!*

Let's examine that answer by looking at the most crucial category of tools that a remote worker uses every day: communication tools. More than a quarter of remote workers view communication as their biggest challenge — even though most organizations today have access to technologies such as chat, videoconferencing, phones, and the internet. How could communication remain a remote worker's biggest challenge?

The answer comes in two forms: unreliable technology and infrequent, incorrect usage.

For example, take one of the most important communication tools: videoconferencing. The first five minutes of the conference call are spent trying to make sure everyone can hear each other. Then right before you say something important that everyone needs to hear, the connection cuts out. Has this ever happened to you?

Remote workers in different time zones often receive meeting invitations for times when they're asleep. Time zones get messed up; they show up to meetings, but there's nobody there. Alternatively, they don't even get invited to the meeting because you forgot that they worked with you because they aren't in the office.

Some of these issues arise from technology choices and the prickly subject of budget. You might be trying to save money in the office by not upgrading to that fiber-optic internet connection. Yet every day, video and VoIP calls are getting garbled, creating delays and frustration for both people in the office and people connecting remotely.

It may not even be an effort to save a dollar. Sometimes people just accept things the way they are. It takes precious time to fix an issue, so if it seems good enough, you run with it.

When workers don't have the communication tools they need, the consequences ripple across the organization. If remote employees struggle to hear on a conference call, or to be heard, or get cut off often, it has a chilling effect on communication. People start talking less. If the whole experience is painful, they'll be less likely to invite others to a videoconference — or to set one up in the first place.

There isn't always an easy fix. At Hugo, because our software is a meeting notes product, we like to stay on top of the latest innovations in meeting hardware.

We've purchased novel products such as Meeting Owl, a 360° conference camera that detects who's speaking and focuses the frame on them. It adapts as the noise moves. When you take a traditional webcam and set it at the end of a table, the experience is somewhat disconnected. Everyone seems far away and stacked on top of each other, and the people at the far end of the room have trouble being heard.

Meeting Owl changes this by putting the camera and microphone in the center of a table, where everyone naturally faces. By dynamically picking up who is speaking and shifting the camera to that person, it creates a much more human experience of being in a meeting. The camera mimics our vision and how a person naturally looks at someone who is speaking.

In his foreword to this book, Eric Yuan of Zoom wrote about why he founded Zoom after working on WebEx at Cisco. WebEx customers were constantly frustrated with the reliability of WebEx; that frustration became the basis for Zoom. Eric realized that nothing else in the software mattered if there were problems with the video and audio.

Reliable communication tools for your remote workers are a worthwhile investment. A couple of extra dollars a month could mean the difference between people who are always ready to collaborate, and those for whom communication is frustrating and painful.

You don't have to be the boss to make an impact here. All too often teams grow complacent with problems with videoconferencing, but just accept it as the status quo. If you are having trouble communicating with others seamlessly, it's your responsibility to step up and ask for better tools.

Videoconferencing isn't the only place where communication tools can make a significant difference. Here's what our virtual collaboration stack looks like at Hugo:

- **Video** – Zoom
- **Chat** – Slack
- **Project management** – Asana & Trello
- **Virtual whiteboard** – Miro
- **Shared meeting notes** – Hugo

Each application in the list above is purpose-built for collaboration. They empower people and remove friction from teamwork.

Chat

Chat apps like Slack, Teams, and Hipchat function like a virtual office, providing communal access to communication. Chat is the perfect place for you to use emojis and GIFs to express those sentiments that are otherwise difficult to convey remotely. And if you don't have it already, you may want to add a casual channel, like a general "Water Cooler" topic.

Project Management

Using a project management app like Asana, Basecamp, monday.com — *there are tons* — is an effective way to stay in sync and help make work more transparent when working remotely. When you watch your notifications and see your team working, commenting, and checking off tasks, it helps build a sense of working together, even though you are physically separated.

Virtual Whiteboard

Video of the other people you're talking to isn't the only visual that can make for a more engaging and effective remote relationship. Virtual whiteboarding software like Miro allows you to bring together text, images, and drawings in a freeform space. It has a creativity-inducing effect, much like in-person whiteboarding. That may sound strange at first, but give it a try. You just might love working with your team in virtual space.

Shared Meeting Notes

When you and your team get together to meet, why not make sure it's the best experience possible? Shared meeting notes allow you to collaborate on agendas in advance, so everyone shows up prepared.

Then, when the meeting is over, it's easy to share what happened so that people who weren't there can stay up to date.

There are also some hardware and infrastructure items you should add to your checklist to enable easy, seamless communication in your organization:

- Fast, reliable internet (both in the office and remotely)
- A headset with a mic to eliminate echoes
- An HD webcam or webcam-enabled laptop
- A door that closes

Get all these tools right, and you're off to a good start. You have laid the foundation for fast and productive remote workers. Now it's time to put those tools to proper use.

24

THE HUMAN FACTOR TO COMMUNICATION

IN THE FYI REMOTE WORK report, remote workers cited a *lack of organic interaction* as a top-five challenge. That probably doesn't come as a surprise. As stated earlier, when you are remote from the rest of your team, everything that happens has to be intentional. There are no serendipitous encounters in the office — no overheard bits of information to seed ideas in your mind.

Opportunities for organic human interaction still abound, though. Not being in the same room as someone does not have to stop you from having a great relationship with them.

Before remote work hit the mainstream, another type of remote interaction had already gained immense popularity in a subsection of the population. It turns out, many people have been practicing working remotely for quite some time. They're quite good at it. You may be too, without even realizing it.

Multiplayer video games, with their complex mechanics, team-based challenges, and real-time communication, offer an analog from which we can learn. Whether you are a gamer or not, you may have heard of people who met their spouse or partner in a video game such as World of Warcraft. Many people who play games together cite their in-game friends as being closer to them than people they know in real life.

This example illustrates how remote relationships can involve the same level of mutual trust, teamwork, camaraderie, and honesty as in-person ones. Here are a few ways you can experience that in your organization.

Build a culture around video

Video connects people with each other. Sometimes this is a video meeting, and other times it's a simple, self-destructing screen recording. Every day, multiple team members share videos like this. It's a much higher bandwidth way to share information than an email, and it's much simpler to do than calling a full-fledged meeting.

Having video on in meetings is a habit that must be cultivated. Not only does it increase the sense of connectedness, but video communication is also often more easily understood than other forms of communication. Participants get to observe each other's facial expressions and body language, both of which are powerful communication signals.

Having video on during meetings also helps people avoid multitasking. This is something many people would never do in an in-person meeting, but they often do on remote calls. Video encourages them to fully connect and communicate with the other people in the meeting.

Have simple, personal interactions

Send a quick chat to just say hello. Ask how their weekend was. When we're in the same space every day, we can take these small, personal interactions for granted. But when you're remote from each other, they can be quite rare. So spend five seconds and send a quick message that doesn't relate to specific work. It goes a long way.

Bring the remote team along for celebrations

Remote team members may not be co-located, but that doesn't mean they cannot celebrate together. One thing we like to do at Hugo is to give an impromptu phone call to each other after a milestone achievement or when something exciting happens.

If everyone at the office is leaving early for happy hour to celebrate, tell remote workers to cut out an hour early and give them $20 for a bottle of wine or something similar. Even if they aren't there in person, they can join in spirit and develop a stronger sense of being part of the team.

25

HOW BEING REMOTE CHANGES TIME AND SPACE

CHRIS MORE, who leads premium subscription services at Mozilla, has sage advice for remote workers: "Create an environment in your remote office that makes you smile each time you step in." Having the right office setup makes remote workers more productive. It helps put us in a professional mindset, ready to tackle the day's challenges.

The perfect remote office isn't as simple as sitting down anywhere you please and opening up your laptop. Unlike in an office — a space that is purpose-built for one thing — working remotely allows people to work from just about anywhere. Even if it is simply their house or apartment, homes are much more multi-use than offices, and as such, aren't optimized for work in the same way.

The environment remote workers work in will affect your company's culture. So in our pursuit of a thriving team culture, we need to also take a look at the remote work environment.

Practice home hygiene

"If you find yourself working in areas that are dedicated to relaxing... your couch, your bedroom, your bathtub..." says Steve Herrick, senior manager of marketing operations at Miro, "it becomes difficult to disconnect when you're fully done for the day." When you work from home, it's very easy to blur the lines between home and office. It is crucial to have a dedicated space that you can go to work that is separate from the space you live in.

Make your hours your own

The clear boundaries required by remote work extend to the time in which you work. What begins as a "make your own hours" policy can quickly turn into an expectation that remote employees are always available. In our experience, it works better for both the business and its team members when there is a clear distinction between expected working hours and time off.

Find a quiet, private place

Especially if you live with other people, and especially if you have a family, you need a place that you can go where you can think, undisturbed. That usually means a room with a door that shuts (bonus points if the door also locks). For some, this place might not be your usual remote work environment, such as a café, a library, or a co-working space.

The perks of being a remote-flower

In a typical work setting, employers make all sorts of contributions to the work environment. Offices don't just have desks and chairs. There are office supplies, snacks, cleaning services, a receptionist, security, parking. In the context of a standard office, leaders view these expenses as the cost of doing business. Remote work can trade off some of the perks above in return for the increased flexibility of being able to dictate your work environment.

However, many companies seeking to cultivate a robust remote culture offer their remote workers similar perks. This can include small things like a coffee shop budget on a corporate card, a gym membership, or a small allocation to be able to spend a certain amount of days in a co-working space as necessary.

To enhance productivity and worker well-being, some companies take it further — sponsoring an ultrafast broadband connection, paying for housekeeping, or helping upgrade a worker's desk to a standing desk.

Don't forget about the remote person's working environment just because you don't see it every day. There's a lot your business can contribute towards that environment that's good for your team culture, and good for your bottom line.

SUMMARY: 10X REMOTE

- Use a full spectrum of communication channels with remote teams, optimizing for high-bandwidth mediums, such as video or voice, while letting people work in the way that is best for them.
- Invest in reliable tools and technology, such as stable videoconferencing and internet, for both remote workplaces and in-person offices.
- Give remote workspaces the same attention that you give office space. Invest in necessary improvements that can pay off with significant gains in productivity.

VII

10X TALENT

By itself, hiring is taxing. And in the recent past, the job market has grown much more competitive. As of this writing, unemployment rates are at multi-year lows in the U.S. and many other countries.

Hiring for a culture fit is even more of a challenge — but it's one that is worthy of your attention. Finding superstar employees who will elevate your company's culture will pay outsized dividends in the long run.

In the not-too-recent past, I worked at a company that marketed its great culture in the hiring process, to great effect. The founders had done their research, and they believed they wouldn't appeal to the best talent unless they used their culture as a differentiator.

So they implemented culture-specific perks, such as giving each person a credit card and permission to spend up to $14 per day on lunch. "We don't want you to have to choose unhealthy food to save money," they said. By making this a major focus, they were able to recruit a team of rock star talent.

Internally, though, the organization was corrupt. Leadership was eventually exposed as having acted unethically — some might say immorally. The cultural values had been adopted at the very top only as a sham to attract top talent.

Even though the leadership at that company didn't really believe in the principle of the culture they created, along the way they had managed to hire a tremendous number of really great people. When it came out that those founders were disconnected from the values they claimed to be proponents of, many people stayed during the turmoil — myself included. The culture was *that* strong.

Following that company's example and giving a candidate a good cultural experience with your company during hiring is challenging. After all, even in a lengthy interview process, they're still only spending a handful of hours with you. There is something, though, that can operate as a stand-in for culture and that can be conveyed incredibly quickly: *purpose*.

Simon Sinek's famous Ted Talk, *How Great Leaders Inspire Action*, discusses how the most important factor for a company to be inspirational is *why* they do what they do. *Why* — the *purpose* of the company's existence — is a core aspect of having a 10X Culture.

Human beings crave meaningfulness in their work, so there's no better motivator than purpose. There is no glue that can hold the team together quite like a common goal. Embracing the deeper purpose for your business, your team, and your work is crucial for building a sustainable and positive team culture.

So in this section of the book, we will look at topics such as culture and purpose, and how to infuse your hiring and coaching practices with them. Then we will discuss a few techniques you can use to bolster your team's interpersonal dynamics.

But first, let's begin at the very beginning, with hiring.

26

THE PEOPLE OF A 10X TEAM

In the beginning of this book, we talked about the heart of a 10X team. Teams that accomplish great feats are:

- adaptable,
- networked, and
- tempo-oriented.

Hiring for these traits can be challenging. And, in our experience, there are aspects to the way that people are traditionally hired for jobs that not only won't help you find the best people, they actually make it harder. Outwardly, the best job candidates are often seen as the ones who are the best prepared and have the most relevant experience. This kind of hire is a "safe bet." But let's break these ideas down for a moment.

Is someone who has spent their entire career in one field or industry likely to be adaptable? Have they been put through the variety of situations necessary to cultivate adaptability as a strength? A less diverse set of experiences suggests the answer might be no.

And when we talk about someone being networked, recall that

we mean that they are both open and connected. Traits such as honesty, work style, and the ability to lift others up are very difficult to detect during the hiring process. After all, you haven't worked with this person yet. One résumé and a handful of interviews can give you a sense of their character, but you really won't know how they work with others until you've actually spent some time with them.

What about the trait of being tempo-oriented? How can you tell if a candidate is able to work efficiently and effectively? So much about the process of trying to get a job goes entirely against the notion of tempo. The schedule of interviews is dictated by the employer; in fact, if you're the one doing the hiring, the entire process is up to you. All of the best contributions to tempo that your candidate can make are blocked because they aren't on your team yet.

Does that mean that you can't hire for culture? Absolutely not. Certainly you can look for evidence of these traits in the stories and answers from your candidate. But there's more you can do, too. Here are some practical ways you can assess candidates for fit with your company culture.

Conduct a culture interview

Don't settle for shoehorning culture assessment into every interview. Instead, many companies dedicate a block of time during the interview process to assessing culture. Having a session specifically geared toward how the candidate thinks about teamwork and what their work style is will be useful later on. Because this is not a skills-based interview, it can be conducted by someone in a different department than you're hiring for.

Here are a few example culture interview questions:

- What gets you excited about coming to work?
- What's the biggest problem in most offices today?
- When was the last time you made a big mistake at work?
- What motivates you?

- What has been the most valuable lesson of your professional career?
- What has been the greatest disappointment of your life to date? How do you handle disappointments?
- Would you rather work alone or as part of a team?

These questions might look like softballs at first, but they're actually quite nuanced. There aren't necessarily right or wrong answers here. Most candidates haven't prepared for questions like these, or if they have, not nearly as much as with more standard interview questions like asking them to describe three strengths and three weaknesses (although that question sometimes also reveals culture quite well).

Vary your interview modes

Mix up your interviews to elicit different cultural traits. One interview could be a formal Q&A-style discussion. Another might be a whiteboard-based workshop focused on fleshing out a single idea. Another could be a coffee, beer, or walk-and-talk to get to know each other better in an informal setting. Both you and the candidate can learn so much more from each other in this way.

Discuss values to affirm them

The topics you bring up during an interview play a large role in shaping your candidate's expectations about the job they have applied for. When planning your interviews, make a list of your team's most important values. Make sure to work them in to your discussions.

Here's a concrete example of a cultural discussion that needs to be had based on the values and vision of your company. Because Hugo is an idea meritocracy, everybody has to be comfortable sharing their ideas. This is especially the case when one person's point of view might conflict with someone else's — even more so because sometimes that person is your boss.

When I was hired, Josh asked me about this. He said that Hugo needs people who have the courage to speak up, and he asked if I would be willing to do so. Many people aren't used to operating in this way, so it was important that he asked that. It's one thing to say that we believe in being an idea meritocracy. It's another thing entirely to set that standard upfront and say, before you are even hired, we want to make sure that you can work in this way.

Operating with radical straightforwardness or engaging in thoughtful disagreements may not be habits that candidates have practiced in other organizations. Even if they are a great fit in this regard, you need to reinforce your values. By bringing them up during the interview process, you are signaling just that. You are saying that these are an important aspect of how you work, and you begin to build a trusting relationship before the job even starts.

Work together before you hire

An incredible hack to hiring the best people is to find a way to do some work together before making the big decisions. One strategy we use often is to ask candidates to come work on a small chunk of work for us. We pay them for their time, and they dig in. This allows us to immediately experience someone's work style and get a much better idea of whether they are going to be a culture fit (not to mention skills fit).

If there aren't any good collaborative projects to work on, sometimes even a small personal project can stand in. This at least lets you observe them going through the process of being brought up to speed, working on something, and debriefing on the results.

Using either of these techniques, you often learn more about a candidate than you will during the entire interview process. I've also seen these techniques reveal new skills and opportunities. At one company, we were hiring a director of operations. We did projects with our two best candidates and both excelled, but in completely different ways. We ended up hiring both: one to run operations, and one to join the sales team and oversee sales operations. If we hadn't worked together before hiring, we may not have realized the potential in front of us.

IN ADDITION to the process of finding the best candidates, there is also the question of which roles and skills are the most important to hire for. In putting so much thought into how we work, we've learned that you have to rethink everything, including the job descriptions and skills you hire for. This has led to seeing new value in people with generalist skill sets as a way to build a more adaptable, fast-moving team.

Why you need cross-functional generalists

In the open culture model that we advocate for throughout this book, information of all kinds can be made useful by everyone within an organization. The way that you move fast with this kind of exchange is by having people who are adaptable and multi-skilled. That kind of person can put to use ideas and innovations that come from the heightened level of shared consciousness throughout the company.

Is there a role for specialists in this kind of organization? Certainly — especially as you scale. Specialists are crucial for accomplishing the deep, difficult work that is required for any groundbreaking product or service. But even those specialists still need to have a cross-functional gene. They need to have a desire to understand aspects of the business beyond their specialty so that they can contribute their deep knowledge wherever it may be useful.

Utilize your extended team

This leads us to the next secret of successful teams: stop trying to do it all in-house. We have already discussed adaptability, and how it is replacing pure efficiency as a way to get ahead in a world of to-the-moon levels of complexity. But there is a way to retain your adaptability while also being incredibly efficient: by bringing in outside help.

For those who are focused on culture, engaging temporary or external team members for specific projects may seem counterintuitive. After all, you don't have time to deeply assess whether they are going to be a culture fit with your company, and they may not have time to assimilate into your culture. There are, however, some serious advantages, culturally and otherwise, to bringing in an army of extra help.

For example, since hiring full-time employees takes careful planning, companies tend to wait until the need for a specific role reaches a critical threshold. In the gap between having a small need for additional help, and having enough of a need to hire someone, others end up picking up the slack. It's inefficient. Contractors can easily fill that gap until the need is great enough to hire someone.

Contractors can also help you move faster, or help free up a team member who has more impactful work to do. One of the reasons that we have been able to move so quickly at Hugo is because we embrace every opportunity to unburden our core team of the tasks that are not the most critical for them to be doing.

We have an in-house expert in data and analytics. So when we discovered gaps in our understanding of user acquisition and retention, the natural first step was to have that person figure out how to connect the data across disparate platforms: Google Analytics, Redshift, our product, and others.

But troubleshooting Google Analytics data is tedious, and it is a common skill and easily defined problem. When you have a mission-critical senior team member doing that kind of thing, what they *aren't* doing is hurting you. So we aim to farm that stuff out. We brought in an analytics guy to help — and he had some great new ideas beyond the scope of his project.

Using this strategy, you will develop over time an arsenal of on-demand services that you can tap into whenever the situation calls for it. That could even be year round, and if it is, you might consider bringing that person on full-time as a remote worker. You will also find that when you have something that needs attention, you can scale it much faster than you could if you allowed yourself to be limited to the resources on hand.

Advice from the outside in

If you truly want to build a 10X Culture, you have to have the willingness to improve as a team and as an individual. Sometimes you are the best person to know something about yourself, and other times you need someone who is able to call you out. One way to unleash this kind of personal and organizational growth — to quickly take dramatic leaps forward — is through the help of outside mentorship and advice.

At Hugo, we have an investor who serves in this role. From time to time, he'll sit down and chat with everyone at the company individually, collecting feedback and hearing everyone's point of view on our main issues. Then he'll go back to the leadership team and deliver recommendations. These include interpersonal tips about how we can lead better and foster a better sense of teamwork, as well as more strategic insights about where we should take the company.

Part philosopher, part therapist, part mentor, he is an invaluable asset to our business in a way that can only be provided as an outsider looking in. He sees everything with fresh eyes, whereas we have grown too accustomed to our work environment to see our blind spots.

Even if there isn't room in the budget to bring in an outside consultant to do this kind of work, almost every organization has access to people who can hold up a mirror to them. Look to your network, your colleagues, and your family. Beyond that, there are many community organizations that provide a great starting point to network or look for mentorship resources.

Outsiders aren't the only ones capable of inspecting your team to see how it can be improved. You can do that yourself, too, with a healthy dose of introspection — and that's the subject of the next section.

27

PERSONALITY AND INTROSPECTION

WHETHER or not people are going to work well together can some-times feel like a crapshoot. Having shared values and good intentions is a great start. But what about all that other stuff that makes us who we are? Everyone has their own distinct personality, and how well personalities get along tends to depend on whether they are compatible.

In my experience, people of all kinds of personalities can have great working relationships with each other. Personalities themselves do not predispose people to conflict. Rather, it tends to be a lack of mutual understanding of each other's work style, a misunderstanding, or the use of the wrong communication method with the wrong person that results in conflict on a team.

The way around this is to examine the way that different people on your team work and to explicitly acknowledge that the same pattern and process that works for some may not work as well for others.

Test your personality

One of the easiest and most enlightening ways to do this is to do a personality test exercise along with the people you work the closest with. Behind everyone's behavior are numerous preferences and patterns. Once you can understand and master these patterns, you can optimize how you work together.

Now you might think that personality tests can be a little bit like a horoscope: the results could apply to anyone if you massage them enough. But whether or not they are entirely accurate is not the point. The point is that this is a group activity focusing on interpersonal dynamics and seeking ways to work better together. That starts all kinds of interesting conversations that would never otherwise occur, and it calls attention to the way that we work together in a way that wouldn't otherwise happen.

Here are the three personality tests I have personal experience with:

- **Myers-Briggs** – The Myers-Briggs Type Indicator is an introspective self-report questionnaire. Its purpose is to indicate differing psychological preferences in how people perceive the world around them and how they make decisions.
- **Clifton StrengthsFinder 2.0** – StrengthsFinder focuses on discovering what you naturally do best. It helps people see how their strongest traits interact with the strengths of the rest of their team. Those who take the test are encouraged to lean into their strengths for exponential results, versus the more common recommendation of working to develop their weaknesses.
- **Facet5** – Facet5 provides "a simple model and common language to explain how people differ in their behavior, motivation and attitudes, and . . . what can be achieved." It is jargon-free, practical, and web-based for easy access.

The insights that you can get about yourself from these tests are amazing resources for personal development. Often, they confirm assumptions you might already have about yourself, your preferences, and the way you work. But even more valuable are the revelations they create in the aggregate for your team.

It's important when doing this kind of formal personality and work-style testing that everyone understands that there are no right or wrong or best or worst answers. Extroverts aren't better than introverts. Activators aren't better than Developers. Whoever you are, and whatever your type is, you can have a positive impact on any team.

One of our core values at Hugo is for everyone to have *strong opinions, weakly held*. We have many team members who are very opinionated — smart people who will passionately advocate for ideas that they think are right. This is great! We want the best ideas out there, but we also want the best ideas to win. So when our leadership did the Facet5 exercise, it helped us counterbalance these natural impulses, enabling more productive discussions — ones where quieter voices in the room still had a microphone.

From free tests to guided workshops that run into the five figures, there are programs and tests out there to match organizations of any size or maturity. To start, we suggest that you have all members of small, close-working teams take the same test. Share the results, and meet to discuss them. It may be helpful to have someone outside of the group act as the facilitator.

While this exercise should help kick-start conversations around how your team can best work together, it does have a shortcoming: it's *one and done*. It's not an ongoing activity that will enable your team to build better processes and communication habits in the long term. That's where retrospectives come in.

28

UPDATE YOUR PERSPECTIVE ON RETROSPECTIVES

IF YOU'VE EVER USED a conference room after a team of developers, you may have noticed something peculiar on the whiteboards. Usually it involves drawings of three faces: happy 🙂, neutral 😐, and sad 🙁. If you discover hieroglyphs such as these, you're witnessing a common practice in agile software development called a *retrospective.*

A retrospective is time spent after a project to reflect not just on its practical success, but also on what did and did not go well from a teamwork and process perspective. The focus is not on how the product or deliverable could be improved, but on how the team can collaborate more effectively to generate better outcomes.

Perhaps it's not surprising that engineers — who frequently refactor code to make it simpler, more effective, and more efficient — were the first group to adopt the mindset of continually refactoring teamwork.

One of the biggest themes in building a 10X culture is developing a team that invests effort like this in collective future success — looking into ways to make the team itself work effectively. To do this, you need to dedicate time and brainpower to looking at how you work and trying to optimize it.

Keep doing what's working

After discussing and listing out how the work has been going so far, the next part of many retrospectives is a *Start, Stop, Continue* exercise:

- What should we start doing?
- What should we stop doing?
- What should we continue doing?

This allows you to make concrete proposals with the team regarding better ways to work together. It's incredibly empowering and useful. Make sure to capture all of these decisions in your meeting notes so you can refer back to them later and see if they have been implemented and how they went.

In his article *Continue, Stop, Start: a new take on retrospectives*, Kuba Niechciał, an engineering manager at Intercom, makes an interesting point about this retrospective structure. Niechciał argues that the traditional prioritization is wrong, and that there is a better order: Continue, Stop, Start. Notice that he suggests that deciding what to keep doing should be the first order of business, while *Start* is moved to the end.

Niechciał writes:

> *Asking what your team should keep doing highlights the positive things that are deep in the culture of your organization that are necessary for future success. To grow sustainably, either as a team or a career, you need to have a strong foundation, and you need to keep focus on it.*

When you start doing something, on the other hand, you have to spin up resources and time to make it work. Starting almost anything requires pulling focus from other activities. Implementing new processes or modes of working too often could have a detrimental effect on your team. That's why this is the last order of business in trying to improve how you work — not the first.

Whether or not you're a developer, we still encourage you to have retrospectives. They may not be tied to a development sprint like they are in agile development, but it's worth stopping and syncing after the completion of a large project, or on a recurring basis, such as weekly, monthly, or quarterly.

You may find it difficult at first to conduct effective retrospective meetings that bring about results. Some participants may even be frustrated by the entire idea of a retrospective, because you're investing time that could be spent *working*. Retrospectives are an important part of teamwork and — like every meeting — at the end everyone involved should feel that something was accomplished. Following these tips for successful retrospectives and avoiding these pitfalls will help you achieve this goal.

Tips for successful retrospectives:

- **Have a moderator** lead the session. The moderator assumes the role of coach and cultural guardian.
- **Have a clear goal** for every retrospective. What are you reviewing, and what are you looking to achieve? This will help the team stay on topic instead of getting sidetracked or using the session as a "suggestion box."
- **Celebrate successes** and congratulate each other. This improves morale and helps motivate everyone to deliver better work.
- **Decide what issues you want to address** early in the meeting. Don't tackle every issue at once. Identify the

most important issues you want to resolve in each session, even if they didn't come up first.

- **Focus on the team and their relationship**, not on the project or product. Retrospectives exist to help the team find ways to work better together.
- **Make retrospectives a judgement-free zone**. When you have an environment where all team members feel at ease, everyone can be involved in the discussion without being afraid of being judged.
- **Identify and note any actionable items or decisions**. Success in retrospection requires not just looking back at what happened, but also determining how to proceed in the future.

Retrospective pitfalls:

- **Don't end a retrospective and never think about it again.** It's important to keep track of previous retrospectives and whether you were able to achieve the goals you set.
- **Don't let the meeting become too negative.** Retrospectives are not there for team members to complain; they're about resolving issues and improving teamwork.
- **Don't go into the meeting unprepared.** It's difficult to come up with spontaneous ideas, so encourage team members to sort their thoughts before the retrospective. You may even want to circulate a collaborative agenda, so the team can start the meeting with agreement on the key issues to discuss.
- **Don't just focus on improvement at all costs** and pressure the team to implement all ideas that arise

during the session. It's unproductive and likely to lead to no real change.

- **Don't let outsiders attend the meeting.**
  Remember that retrospectives should focus on building the team's internal relationships. Having an outsider (such as an executive) in the room may make it difficult for the team to openly discuss mistakes or concerns.

When you hire for culture fit, you create a more cohesive, value-driven team. And by paying attention to how you work, you can continually improve your work styles and foster positive relationships with everyone around you. The people around you are your biggest asset. And now you're ready to take each other to the next level.

SUMMARY: 10X TALENT

- The hiring process poses challenges for detecting culture fit. Use a culture interview or work together on a short project as part of your culture assessment.
- Leveraging outside help, such as freelancers, contractors, and advisers, is a good way to energize your company with new skills and resources.
- Have small teams take a test such as Myers Briggs, CliftonStrengths 2.0, or Facet5 in order to start a discussion about ways to work more effectively together.
- Update how you think about retrospectives, which help you review what went well in a project and what didn't. Determine what to continue doing, what to stop doing, and what to start doing — in that order.

CONCLUSION

You might be enthusiastic about the ideas presented in this book. I hope you are, because I know from experience how transformative they can be.

But you may also be thinking, "I can see how this works for a team of five, ten, or 20, but mine is much bigger. How are we supposed to make culture work for a team of thousands?"

Or perhaps you're worried that your team is too rigid. Too *set in its ways*. Resistance to change is hard to overcome, and you have enough to do as it is.

Embrace those concerns and lean into them. If you feel that improving your team culture is going to be difficult, you likely have the most to gain from change.

Building a strong culture in a more established organization can be more challenging, but it has been done time and time again. As you've come along in this journey, you've seen how companies like Atlassian and Zoom managed to create and maintain a strong culture despite growing into massive organizations. We've also looked at teams like the Joint Task Force in Iraq and the Apollo 11 mission.

We picked these examples because they represent some of the

most unlikely candidates for 10X Culture — major national and global projects that involve stakeholders and actors on all sorts of levels and from varied backgrounds, with the added complexities of being handicapped by government procedures and being time-bound in addressing a threat to human lives. Teams of any size and composition — even large and rigid ones — can transform too.

If you're ready to take the first step, where should you begin?

Start with the people around you — those who you trust and work most closely with. Bring your ideas to them. Share books like this one, and the other's we've mentioned. Tell them you would like to discuss how you work together, and see if there are ways that would not only make you more productive, but also more engaged with your work.

When you have some buy-in, don't rush it. Proposing too many changes at once might cause too big of a shock. Try picking just a handful of ideas — or maybe just one — and giving it a test run. Agree to try, say, the practices of being an idea meritocracy for a month. Or that everyone is going to share their meeting notes on Slack to increase transparency.

Win the group over by deciding that you all will talk about how it went. You'll decide together whether you want to keep going. It might surprise you how excited your team gets at the idea of not just working harder to get better results, but thinking about ways to work better entirely.

Team culture is the greatest enabler. It binds people to each other. It motivates. It allows you to harness the unseeable electricity that makes a group of humans able to accomplish far more than they could ever do as individuals.

So get started on your 10X Culture today.

And shoot for the moon.

APPENDIX A - CUSTOMER INTERVIEW TEMPLATE

Introduction

Thank you and explain why you're talking

- Thanks for agreeing to participate in this session, and thank you for being a (company) customer.
- **Before we begin: I would like to record this call for research purposes. Is that okay with you?**
- I'm (name), one of (company and role), and I'm mainly responsible for (reason why we're talking today).
- This workstream is part of a regular research exercise that I conduct, speaking to different people across our user segments (ranging from small, free teams to large, paying teams).
- It helps us to understand what we're doing right that shouldn't change, and where there is room for us to provide more value and solve more problems to improve the way we all work together.

Part 1: Background

Background on their company

- What does your company do?
- What do you specifically do, and who do you work with?
- What is your organizational structure like?

How they interact with your company/product

- How long have you been using us?
- Who do you use our product with?
- What was the initial motivator that sparked an evaluation of (company)?
- What problem did you need to solve, and why did you think we would solve it?
- What were you using to solve this problem before trying us?
- What is the general purchasing/adoption process like at your company?

Part 2: Value

Benefits

- What do you get out of (company) today? You initially signed up for (reason):
- Did our product/service do what you thought it would do?
- Did it do more, or something different altogether that you realized you needed?

Commitment

- Do you think you have committed to (company), or it is still being evaluated by the business?
- Do you recall the turning point where you/your team realized that (company) was worth committing to from a (your unique value proposition) standpoint?
- Help me understand the reasons for your current team size
- You have (number of employees) employees today.
- Is that your company / department / project size?
- Do you anticipate this remaining unchanged, or growing in the future?
- How critical is (company) to your daily work? What other companies would you compare us to?

Part 3: Decision-Specific Questions

The questions in this part of the conversation relate to whatever decisions we are making soon, such as our product roadmap

Part 4: General Discussion

Open-ended questions to provoke topics you may not have covered

- What challenges do you have at work that you would like to see us solve?
- What aspects of the product would you like to see improved?

RESOURCES

Books

Blink: The Power of Thinking Without Thinking
Malcolm Gladwell

The Culture Code
Daniel Coyle

Drive: The Surprising Truth About What Motivates Us
Daniel Pink

Everything's an Offer: How to do more with less
Robert Poynton

The Power of Vulnerability
Brené Brown

Principles: Life and Work
Ray Dalio

Steve Jobs
Walter Isaacson

The Storytelling Animal: How Stories Make Us Human by
Jonathan Gottschall

*Team of Teams: New Rules of Engagement for a Complex
World*
Gen. Stanley McChrystal, Tantum Collins, David Silver-
man, and Chris Fussell

What Got You Here Won't Get You There
Marshall Goldsmith

Yes to the Mess: Surprising Leadership Lessons from Jazz
Frank Barrett

TED Talks

How language shapes the way we think
Lea Boroditsky

How to turn a group of strangers into a team
Amy C. Edmondson

Other

2016 *Letter to Shareholders* On the philosophy of "disagree
and commit" by Jeff Bezos

Continue, Stop, Start: a new take on retrospectives
Article by Kuba Niechciał

Meeting Owl
A 360° meeting conference camera

Open, a blog about the future of work
Atlassian (www.atlassian.com/open)

The Remote Work Report
FYI (usefyi.com/remote-work-report)

ABOUT THE AUTHORS

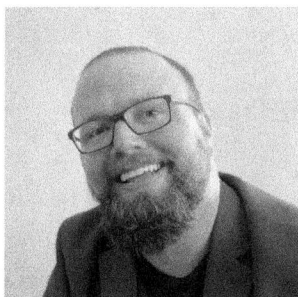

Rob Lennon

Product Education Lead at Hugo

Rob Lennon is Product Education Lead at connected meetings notes company Hugo. His experience spans a diverse 16 years in retail and SaaS startups across healthcare, mar-tech, and ad-tech, and productivity software sectors. His articles and quotes have been featured in publications such as Thrive Global, AdAge, MediaPost, The Drum, TecHR Series, and BizReport.

Having almost died eight times — most infamously while saving a baby porpoise in the frigid waters of Point Reyes, seven miles from a great white shark breeding ground — Rob has a daily appreciation for the simple stuff that life brings to him.

Josh Lowy

Co-Founder and CEO at Hugo

Native to Australia and based in San Francisco, Josh is most excited about the era of innovation we are continuing to experience at work — while the last decade of progress energized us as consumers, it is now our tools and teams at work that are riding a wave of competition and progress. He's seen firsthand the incredible power of decentralized decision-making and distributed teams, where every member is empowered by information and given the autonomy to execute.

However there is still one major barrier - meetings. Meetings shape teamwork and yet they remain largely unchanged and disconnected. Those that miss a meeting don't benefit from what was discussed and actioned, and the software that powers our workflows are being left behind, at the conference room door. That led to the creation of Hugo — connected meeting notes software — with the purpose of uniting meetings with the people and tools that we rely on every day.

Previously a product manager at Westfield Retail Solutions where Josh built wayfinding solutions for brands to convert online shopper intent into offline purchases. He studied at the University of Technology in Sydney, Australia.

Darren Chait

Co-Founder and COO at Hugo

Also an Australian native, Darren Chait leads the growth and operations side of Hugo.

Solving some of the pain around meetings is a cause close to Darren's heart. Prior to founding Hugo, he was a lawyer at one of Australia's largest law firms — he attended meetings for a living! Sharing his frustration with a close friend, now co-founder, the two decided to build Hugo to re-think meetings based on the new way that we work.

Today, Darren regularly writes and speaks at leading events about trends in the way we work and the impact that SaaS is having on teams. He and the Hugo team are on a mission to reconnect the way we meet to the way we work – for themselves and the thousands of teams powered by Hugo.

Darren earned his Bachelor's degrees in Commerce and Law — at the University of New South Wales and a Graduate Diploma of Legal Practice from the College of Law.

POWER YOUR 10X CULTURE

Hugo - Connected Meeting Notes
Centralized, searchable meeting notes that connect with your
favorite tools.

Learn more at **www.hugo.team**

ONE LAST THING

I'm asking for a favor.

If you took something away from this book — if you made notes, if you questioned old assumptions, or you were inspired to work differently — I'm hoping you will take another step forward.

Give a copy of *10X Culture* to someone else. Ask them to read it. Let them know it's possible to be more motivated and connected to each other and the work we do.

Anyone can download this book free at: **www.hugo.team/10x**

Please help spread the word,

Rob

www.ingramcontent.com/pod-product-compliance
Lightning Source LLC
LaVergne TN
LVHW051404080426
835508LV00022B/2963